Growing through Encouragement
a user-friendly guide to 1 Thessalonians

Growing through Encouragement

a user-friendly guide to
1 Thessalonians

Roger Carswell

Bryntirion Press

© Roger Carswell, 1997
First published 1997
Reprinted 2000
ISBN 1 85049 128 3

Cover photo & design: burgum boorman ltd.

Published by the
Bryntirion Press
Bryntirion, Bridgend CF31 4DX, Wales, UK
Printed by Creative Print & Design (Wales) Ltd.
Ebbw Vale, Mon., Wales, UK

Contents

Dedicated to the late Professor Verna Wright, and his wife Esther, who did in person for me what the apostle Paul did for the Thessalonians. With great patience and Christian love, they carefully took me under their wing, and over many years encouraged me by word and life to walk in the ways of the Lord. I saw their work of faith, labour of love and patience of hope, and wanted to imitate their example.

Foreword

Commentaries on 1 Thessalonians abound, but this volume is unique.

First, it was written by a gifted evangelist whose experiences in reaching the lost touch the truths Paul put into this epistle. This book came from the battlefield, not the ivory tower. It doesn't just instruct the mind; it inspires and challenges the heart. That's the kind of commentary we need today.

Second, it was written by a man who believes in the church and has devoted his life to helping churches become all that God wants them to be. First Thessalonians focuses on the local church, its opportunities, problems and resources; and Roger Carswell knows these subjects well. Like a tender physician, he diagnoses the disease and dispenses the medication, and that's what makes churches grow and prosper.

I could go on, but I'll mention a third unique feature: these pages are filled with spiritual nuggets for busy Christian workers. An anointed communicator, Roger knows how to 'set the table' so that the food is both appetizing and nourishing. He is true to the Scriptures and seeks to exalt Jesus Christ alone. As you read, you will find yourself 'mining' precious treasures that you can share with others in your own ministry.

I pray that this book will have a wide and fruitful ministry, and I hope that others like it will follow.

Warren W. Wiersbe
Distinguished Professor of Preaching
Grand Rapids Baptist Seminary
Grand Rapids, Michigan, USA

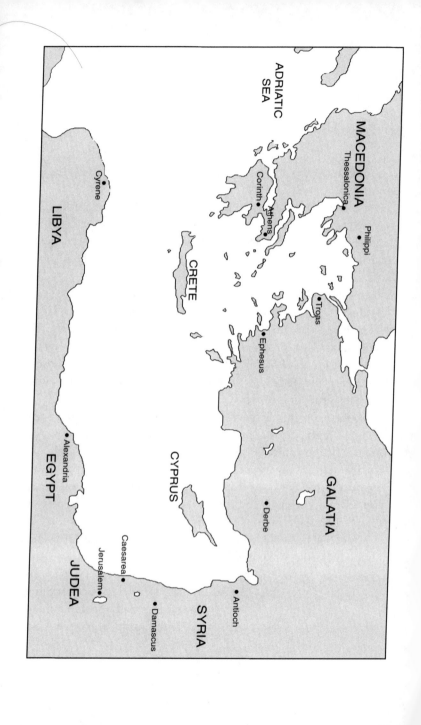

Preface

To each of us, individual verses or books of the Bible stand out as our favourites, or our most treasured. I certainly have such portions, but to tell you which they are, and why, would fill another little book.

However, you have probably guessed—I love 1 Thessalonians. It is so encouraging. To think of all that was accomplished in those Thessalonian Christians, is in itself cheering. If that alone is not enough, Paul's words of encouragement, written to stir up the sense of hope in the hearts of the young, persecuted converts are like a sweet-tasting tonic.

At times in 1 Thessalonians it is as if we are provided with an X-ray into the innermost being of the apostle Paul and, indeed, every true Christian. The insights into the very heart of the Lord God stand out in this little letter.

My prayer is that as you work through 1 Thessalonians using *Growing through Encouragement* you will have a look afresh into your own heart, and in doing so, recommit yourself to his royal service with a new sense of love, faith and hope, until the time of his glorious return.

I am grateful to my good friend Mr David Harding, pastor of Milnrow Evangelical Church, Rochdale, for his helpful comments on the manuscript, and also to my ever loving, ever patient, ever helpful, parents for keeping true to their lifetime work of correcting my grammar and improving the flow of words. I am grateful for the willing sacrifices that my wife Dot, and children Emma, Benjamin, Hannah-Marika, and Jonathan have made, as I've worked over an open Bible with a word processor. I pray that God would more than abundantly make up for any losses that they may have felt. Emma's editing skills have been given plenty of scope for practice as she put the finishing touches to this manuscript.

Chapter one

A church is conceived

Acts 17:1–10

Now when they had passed through Amphipolis and Apollonia, they came to Thessalonica, where there was a synagogue of the Jews. Then Paul, as his custom was, went in to them, and for three Sabbaths reasoned with them from the Scriptures, explaining and demonstrating that the Christ had to suffer and rise again from the dead, and saying, 'This Jesus whom I preach to you is the Christ.' And some of them were persuaded; and a great multitude of the devout Greeks, and not a few of the leading women, joined Paul and Silas.

But the Jews who were not persuaded, becoming envious, took some of the evil men from the marketplace, and gathering a mob, set all the city in an uproar and attacked the house of Jason, and sought to bring them out to the people. But when they did not find them, they dragged Jason and some brethren to the rulers of the city, crying out, 'These who have turned the world upside down have come here too. Jason has harboured them, and these are all acting contrary to the decrees of Caesar, saying there is another king—Jesus.' And they troubled the crowd and the rulers of the city when they heard these things. So when they had taken security from Jason and the rest, they let them go.

Then the brethren immediately sent Paul and Silas away by night to Berea. When they arrived, they went into the synagogue of the Jews.

Be honest! Have you ever pried into someone else's mail, to read their private letter? We'll not discuss now the morality of doing that, but instead we will share in the blessing of nosing into a letter written by Paul to a group of Christians living in the city of Thessalonica. What we are about to do is most commendable, for Paul himself wrote: 'I charge you by the Lord that this epistle be read to all the holy brethren' (1 Thess. 5:27), so we are not in fact peering into a private letter.

Paul was a pattern-saint for all believers. He was not sinless; only Christ is that. Nevertheless, there is much we can learn from his life of dedication, devotion and discipline. His sacrifice and suffering for the cause of his beloved Saviour is an example to us all. Paul was used by the Holy Spirit to pen words which are preserved in our Bible today (2 Pet. 3:15). We are going to study what could well have been Paul's first letter to a young church—his first letter to the Thessalonian Christians, which was almost certainly written between 50 and 51 AD.

Thessalonica was a major city for the Romans, named by Alexander the Great, after his sister. Today it is the second largest city in Greece. At the time of the New Testament, it was the principal metropolis of Macedonia, being situated on a main trading route. The book of Acts says that Paul preached in the synagogue of Thessalonica for the space of just three Sabbath days, that being some time between two and four weeks. This is probably referring only to his time in the synagogue as Phil. 4:16 (and 1 Thess. 2:9), imply that Paul was in Thessalonica much longer, if you include his work with the Gentiles. First he preached in the synagogue of the Jews where he used the Old Testament to build a bridge to Jesus Christ. As all the Bible prophesies, portrays or points to Christ, one can preach Jesus from any part of the Bible, for the Bible speaks of Christ. (See Luke 24:26,27 and Acts 8:35.) Therefore, the first converts would have a grasp of the Scriptures as a whole.

Paul kept to the main theme and essential purpose of his visit. He did not speak of himself, but of Christ, 'explaining and demonstrating that the Christ had to suffer and rise again from the dead . . .' (v.3). Despite the ever-present temptation to stray

12

from the basics of the gospel, Paul refused such distracting by-paths. Jesus was the focus of his heart, and therefore of his message. Proclaiming Christ draws crowds and provokes controversy, as indeed the Thessalonians were to find. Despite Paul's awareness of this, he did not water down his message to please the crowds.

The gospel is said to be 'to the one, an aroma of death to death, and to the other the aroma of life to life' (2 Cor. 2:16). Hence where Christ is preached there will be both conversions and confrontations, some souls saved and others angered. This is exactly what happened in Thessalonica. When Paul preached the gospel there, some people repented and believed the gospel, and others bitterly opposed not only Paul, but also Christ himself (see Acts 9:5).

A Christian is a 'persuaded' person—he or she has been persuaded of the need to find peace with God, and of the truth of the gospel that 'Christ died for our sins according to the Scriptures, and that He was buried, and that He rose again on the third day' (1 Cor. 15:3-4). Each Christian has believed on the Lord Jesus Christ and been saved.

Notice the three words: 'explaining', 'demonstrating' and 'persuaded' (vv.3,4). We find the same ideas in Acts 28, where Paul towards the end of his life 'explained', 'testified' and 'persuaded' people concerning Christ. No doubt Paul had matured in his faith and grown in his understanding of the Lord Jesus, but his concern remained firmly founded on the commission, 'to go into all the world and preach the gospel to every creature' (Mark. 16:15). Christian growth did not lead to a lessening of evangelistic zeal. Paul was thorough, deep and theological in his preaching, but he never became too sophisticated for 'the simplicity which is Christ' (2 Cor. 11:3). He began and finished his ministry well.

Paul's stay in Thessalonica was short but significant. Centuries before, as Abraham travelled he put up his tent and erected an altar. When he moved on, the altar remained as a permanent witness to the fact that a man of God had dwelt and worshipped there. Similarly, when Paul had to flee the city because of persecution,

13

there was a permanent testimony left—men and women had been converted to Christ. Do you pray that wherever you go, you would leave an abiding witness to the glory of God? A friend who worked first in city-cleansing, but now serves as a pastor of a growing church, testifies to the fact that in every place he has lived, people were converted to Christ through his witness.

Paul was accused of turning the world upside down. Actually, the world is the wrong way up, and needs to get the right side up, and we are the people, under God, to do it! Dr Walter Maier said, 'Every century of history is marked by deep sorrows which have come from blind obedience to false leaders.' Christianity has always moved on despite persecution and difficulty. The opposition to Paul was so great that he was sent over 50 miles away to Berea. (Paul was going to face persecution there too). In the book of Acts, we read of Paul at times escaping opposition (Acts 9:23-25) and at other times, staying resolutely in the same place to face trouble if need be (Acts 21:13). Sensitivity to the Lord's leading is needed at such times. The pattern is that Paul escaped when his presence brought trouble to others, but stayed when he alone was the focus of hatred.

However, the work in Thessalonica had been remarkably blessed. Many had been converted, and Paul had a great love for these new converts. Aware that persecution can lead to stumbling (Matt. 13:21), Paul wrote to the Thessalonian church to encourage them. The Oxford English Dictionary defines 'encourage' as 'to inspire with courage, animate, inspirit, to embolden, to stimulate, to promote the growth of.' 1 Thessalonians is bursting with hope and encouragement. If you are feeling low because the pressure has been increasing and the obstacles to joyful Christian living seem mountainous, then 1 Thessalonians is for you. There is plenty here which will bless, restore and even thrill your soul, lifting you to heights above any difficulty, and helping you to keep your focus on Christ. Let us then begin our study of it.

Chapter two

A church is born

1 Thessalonians 1

Verses 1-2
Paul, Silvanus, and Timothy, To the church of the Thessalonians in God the Father and the Lord Jesus Christ: Grace to you and peace from God our Father and the Lord Jesus Christ. We give thanks to God always for you all, making mention of you in our prayers.

The three men who wrote this letter were accused of turning the world upside down! One of the methods they used was to write letters. Thank God they did. Letters can inform, explain, challenge, and encourage. This letter is primarily one of encouragement. In all its five chapters there is not even one rebuke. The aim all through is to strengthen young believers who are being persecuted. Despite having to leave them, Paul's heart and his prayers were still with them. Hence his letter, written to encourage this group of persecuted, young believers.

Incidentally, letters, or even just a postcard, can still be a powerful means of communicating vital truth to people. They can be a means of spiritually investing in the life of someone far from you, and can make a lasting impact for good. (See Prov. 25:25).

I wonder what you would say to a struggling believer if you really wanted to encourage him or her? Together with his friends Silvanus and Timothy, Paul reminded the Thessalonians of the Second Coming of Christ. Each chapter in this letter ends with the thought and theme of Christ's imminent return. Don't be put

15

off by varying human devised systems about the Second Coming, but be encouraged by the fact that he is coming again. Often what appear to be theological problems are really theological pearls. F. B. Meyer in his *Our Daily Homily* writes: 'We should never lose this spirit of eager longing and waiting . . . It lifts above the darkness of the present age; links the present with the great future; comforts us amid bereavement with the hope of speedy re-union; quickens us to watchfulness and consecration by the thought of the shortening of our opportunities; leads us to purify ourselves as He is pure, to gird our loins and trim our lamps.' The Second Coming of Christ also reminds us that history is going somewhere, and we need not despair when forces unfriendly to Christ seem to be gaining the upper hand.

G. Harding Wood in his short expository work, *St Paul's First Letter*, suggests an outline of the 1 Thessalonians which I have changed and expanded a little:

In the light of the Second Coming of Christ, we should dispose of:
- **substitutes in the heart** – chapter 1
- **slackness in our service** – chapter 2
- **schism in our fellowship** – chapter 3
- **sensuality in our behaviour** – chapter 4:1-7
- **sorrow in our minds** – chapter 4:8-18
- **sin in our lives** – chapter 5

There is no sense of criticism in these themes, only a continuing and loving challenge to the Christians whom Paul has grown to love. Each chapter has him affirming his great affection for these believers:

- **'We give thanks to God for you' (1:2)**
- **'Affectionately longing for you' (2:8)**
- **'When I could no longer endure it, I sent to know your faith' (3:5)**
- **'We exhort you' (4:1,10)**
- **'We urge you' (5:11)**

Paul begins by greeting these young Christians. In all his pastoral letters, Paul desires grace and peace for the readers. (This is the New Testament counterpart of Numbers 6:23-26, and is not merely a wish, but a blessing.) The greeting in 1:1 is typical of Paul's opening lines to believers (see 1 Cor. 1:3; Eph. 1:12; Phil. 1:2). God's grace is the basis of all our Christian experience. We are saved, not by our works of righteousness, but according to God's grace and mercy to us. Grace is receiving what we do not deserve; mercy is not receiving what we do deserve—God's condemnation for our sins. Peace is that unruffled quietness which defies the crashing, crushing circumstances of life. Peace comes only through resting on God's Word and promises.

Paul was truly a man of prayer. He prayed systematically, 'making mention' of many situations and churches. He loved people and one of the greatest evidences of this is that he prayed for them. Through prayer it is possible to be involved in and even change the life and work of others, even though we may be miles from them. Even when he was not presently worried about some catastrophe or sin Paul still constantly prayed for Christian friends. How often do we merely turn to prayer in an emergency?

Paul frequently asked others to pray for him. He could do so because he prayed for them. We need each other, and we need the Lord. Let us become and remain people of prayer. Then many will be giving thanks—for many are being blessed—because many people are praying (see 2 Cor. 1:11). I personally, keep a prayer-diary in which I have lists of people, churches, evangelistic works and missions all of whom I seek to pray for—some each week, others each day. I recommend the idea.

1:3

Remembering without ceasing your work of faith, labour of love, and patience of hope in our Lord Jesus Christ in the sight of our God and Father.

The Thessalonian Christians were marked by their 'work of faith, labour of love and patience of hope'. What a contrast to the church in Ephesus who worked, laboured and had patience, but without faith, hope and love (see Rev. 2:2). It is all too easy to continue in the routine of Christianity, but without faith, hope and love this becomes a rut. What powerless Christianity is this! Frankly, it is nauseating in the sight of God. Thankfully, the Thessalonians were quite different.

The way a person works is very revealing. Some work because of fear of punishment, others only for financial reward, still others out of a sense of grim duty. Working because of faith makes a humble worker—we acknowledge that the Lord is the only one who can give the increase to our labours. We can see the faith of the Thessalonian Christians expressed throughout the letter (see 1:8,9; 2:13; 3:5-8).

Love makes an industrious worker—our motivation is our sheer, grateful love for Christ. It is his work, not ours. There are examples of the love of the Thessalonian Christians strewn through the chapters of this letter (see 3:6,12-13; 4:9-11; 5:12-13).

Hope makes a persevering worker—we know that we shall reap if we sow and do not lose heart. Practical illustrations of steadfast hope are seen in 1:6-7,9-10; 4:13-18; 5:8-11, 23-24. Alexander the Great, setting out on his campaigns divided his possessions among friends. Someone asked, 'Are you keeping nothing for yourself?' 'Oh, yes,' he replied, 'I have kept my hopes.'

Faith, hope and love are like the three legs of a stool, and need to be kept strong and balanced.

Christianity is not a work to be endured for duty's sake, but rather a Person to be served for love's sake. There are times when as individuals, we need to take stock spiritually and ask ourselves whether our motivation in Christian service is from a love for the Lord and the lost, or a love of self.

1:4-10

Knowing, beloved brethren, your election by God. For our gospel did not come to you in word only, but also in power, and in the Holy Spirit and in much assurance, as you know what kind of men we were among you for your sake. And you became followers of us and of the Lord, having received the word in much affliction, with joy of the Holy Spirit, so that you became examples to all in Macedonia and Achaia who believe. For from you the word of the Lord has sounded forth, not only in Macedonia and Achaia, but also in every place. Your faith toward God has gone out, so that we do not need to say anything. For they themselves declare concerning us what manner of entry we had to you, and how you turned to God from idols to serve the living and true God, and to wait for His Son from heaven, whom He raised from the dead, even Jesus who delivers us from the wrath to come.

Paul's greeting to the church is over. He now immediately proceeds, in verses four to ten, to trace the path of the gospel in the lives of the believers at Thessalonica:

1. **Election by God's grace (v.4)**
2. **Assurance of salvation (v.5)**
3. **Receiving the word (v.6)**
4. **Persecution with joy (v.6)**
5. **Witness in deeds (v.7)**
6. **Witness with words (v.8)**
7. **Separation from the old life (v.9)**
8. **Expectation of the return of Jesus Christ (v.10)**

The aim of the letter is encouragement. These new Christians made good progress as they became established in Christ. Though we cannot fathom the mystery, it is a great comfort to know that God chose us before the very foundation of the world. I regularly thank the Lord that I was born in a country and family, and was later in a situation, where I would hear the gospel. I am engraved in the palm of his hand, and therefore am very secure in his tender care.

Notice, in verse 4, how Paul calls these people 'beloved brethren'. 'Brethren' is Paul's favourite name for Christians, both male and female. It is used over sixty times in his letters and at least twenty-seven times in 1 & 2 Thessalonians. It is clear that Paul really loved these young believers.

Verse 5
For our gospel did not come to you in word only, but also in power, and in the Holy Spirit and in much assurance, as you know what kind of men we were among you for your sake.

Paul does not rebuke the Thessalonian Christians for anything in this little letter. They are being persecuted, and he is wanting to encourage them. He builds on what they already knew (see also

2:1,2,5,11; 3:3,4; 4:2; 5:2). They certainly knew what he was like as a man, and he could challenge them from his own life-style, which was exemplary. The preacher matters more than the sermon, though the message preached can tell us a lot about the preacher! The gospel was preached with power, in much assurance and in the Holy Spirit. Power is not dependent upon natural ability or eloquence. It is a work of God's Spirit which gives authority and authenticity to that which is being proclaimed. True power will bring glory to God, rather than to a particular individual. Power is not worked up, but prayed down. It is not always visible, but it is promised. Power in proclaiming the gospel comes when there has been much prayer, as well as a faithfulness in life and message.

When the gospel comes with power, it is evidenced in:

> 1. **conversions (1:5)**
> 2. **willingness to suffer (2:14)**
> 3. **holiness (4:3)**
> 4. **stirring up of hope (1:10)**
> 5. **binding together in love (2:17,20; 3:6,12)**

This is the first time we read the phrase 'as you know'. It is frequently found throughout the letter (see 2:1,5,11; 3:3,4; 4:2; 5:2). As Paul writes, he relives his experiences with them. His words matched his actions.

Verse 6
And you became followers of us and of the Lord, having received the word in much affliction, with joy of the Holy Spirit.

In our cosy Western Christianity, we imagine that joyful Christianity is trouble-free. Paul had warned the Thessalonian Christians that this would not be so (3:4; see also Acts 14:22). All who live godly in Christ Jesus will suffer persecution (2 Tim. 3:12), but that does not mean that our joy will vanish away. In fact, the opposite is true—see Matthew 5:10. When Paul and Silas were in prison in Philippi, just before arriving in Thessalonica, they had been beaten and abused, but even at midnight they were still praising God (Acts 16:25). Their testimony was bright even under the darkness of persecution. Joy is the overflowing of a heart which is right with God, not the bubbly happiness of a moment of passing pleasure. It is joy created by the Spirit.

Take a moment to trace the theme of praise under persecution, and look up: Lk. 6:22,23; Acts 5:40,41; 13:50-52; Rom. 5:3; 2 Cor. 7:4; 8:2; 1 Pet. 4:12,13.

'Affliction' spoken of here, is that which assails a person from the outside. In contrast, the 'joy of the Holy Spirit' is that quiet assurance pervading us inside. Suffering must not be allowed to make us bitter, but better, as we turn difficulties into opportunities to glorify God, by taking them as from him, and quietly trusting in the fact that he knows best. Troubles and unworthy reactions can reveal where true confidences have been.

Christians must *never* idolize other believers, no matter how greatly used of God they may have been. Of course, we must follow other Christians as the Thessalonians followed Paul, in the areas where they follow Christ, and in so doing we are following the Lord himself. Don't wear the off-the-peg ideas of others, but take your beliefs and standards from the Lord himself, by reading his Word. Learn from others, by all means, but most of all learn of Christ.

Verses 7-8
So that you became examples to all in Macedonia and Achaia who believe. For from you the word of the Lord has sounded forth, not only in Macedonia and Achaia, but also in every place. Your faith toward God has gone out, so that we do not need to say anything.

22

What wonderful examples these young Christians were! News of them spread far and wide. Christians either encourage or discourage one another. What a joy it is to hear of Christians and churches in other places which are doing well. (Do we similarly rejoice when these fellowships are nearer to hand, or do we grow jealous?) The spreading of positive news about Christians helps the spreading of the news about Christ.

The Thessalonian Christians were receivers (2:13) and transmitters (1:8). What we receive from God, we are to pass on to others, and in so doing, we are doubly blessed. God gives, and we give, and as we give, he gives more abundantly. We can never out-give God.

God still blesses nations, churches, fellowships and individuals of whom it can be said, 'from you sounded forth the word of the Lord'. There are many ways this may be done—by preaching, writing, practically helping through finance and personnel, as well as by showing acts of faith, love and hope. If the Lord's will for our lives is to stay on our home territory, then we ought to be deeply involved in the missionary endeavour of those who have gone into all the world to preach the gospel. It is always more blessed to give than receive, and to 'give' the gospel to someone brings great cheer.

Verses 9-10
For they themselves declare concerning us what manner of entry we had to you, and how you turned to God from idols to serve the living and true God, and to wait for His Son from heaven, whom He raised from the dead, even Jesus who delivers us from the wrath to come.

God made human beings in his own image but there is a constant tendency for us to make gods in our own image. In turn, we then become like the gods we worship. The second of the Ten

23

Commandments speaks against this (Exod. 20:4-6). The true and living God cannot exist side by side with idolatry, as is illustrated by the demise of Dagon (1 Sam. 5:1-7). Satan must bow to Jesus. By turning to God the power of idols is overcome in the lives of people who have lived with wrong values and priorities. The Thessalonian Christians had done this. Our God is true and living, whereas idols are untrue and dead. They do not communicate, nor can they help in time of need (see Ps. 115:4-8). How many Bible examples of this can you recall? Notice three attitudes shown by the Thessalonians in dealing with idols: turning, serving and waiting. They set a pattern which all Christians have followed; we too, have turned to serve, and to wait for the Lord Jesus to come from heaven.

In Christian experience there will be renunciations. Most of us have been guilty of making idols which dominate our devotion, duties, decisions, delights and dislikes. We can never really renounce them until we have confidently established a right relationship with God through Jesus.

There is an interesting link between the beginning and end of this chapter (vv.3,10). Evidence of their 'work of faith' is seen in that they 'turned to God from idols'; proof of their 'labour of love' is seen in the fact that they 'served the living and the true God'; and finally we can see their 'patience of hope' in their willingness to 'wait for His Son from heaven'.

Paul encourages the Christians by reminding them of the second coming of Christ. Each chapter in this letter ends on the note of Christ's glorious return to this earth in might and majesty. There was a three-day wait for the resurrection of the once crucified Christ; today we are waiting for his return. What a source of comfort for all suffering or persecuted believers—Christ is risen; Christ is coming again! He will deliver us from the hostile powers of this world and from the presence of Satan. Let us be often comforted by the thought that Christ is coming again.

With that blessèd hope before us,
    Let our joyful songs be sung;
Let the mighty advent chorus
    Onward roll from tongue to tongue.
        Christ is coming!
    Come, Lord Jesus, quickly come!

John Ross Macduff, 1818–95

Chapter three

A church grows

1 Thessalonians 2

Verse 1

For you yourselves know, brethren, that our coming to you was not in vain.

Chapter 1 of this letter focuses on how the church of Thessalonica was born, but chapter 2 centres on how it was nurtured. In chapter 1 Paul is the evangelist, in chapter 2 Paul is the pastor. After faithful preaching, there is faithful pastoring.

This chapter contains insights into the manner of life of the apostle Paul. He was characterized by integrity, devotion and total commitment to Christ, and this was harnessed to a life of discipline. Hudson Taylor said, 'A person may be dedicated and devoted, but if ill-disciplined will be useless.' Inward dedication has to be driven by a love for Christ and disciplined choices concerning the priorities of the use of our time, energy, talents and money.

Even though Paul had only been in the city of Thessalonica for a comparatively short time he founded a church there. Paul's time had been fruitful, because he had been faithful. Paul, Silvanus (=Silas) and Timothy had seen souls saved, and a church established. It is not wrong to ask the Lord to give us souls. (See Romans 10:1). We pray and long for abiding fruit for our labours. Everywhere we go, we should pray that 'our coming was not in vain'. The same phrase occurs again in chapter 3:5, where Paul expresses his concern that possibly the Tempter (*i.e.* Satan) had tempted the believers, undermining his efforts on their behalf. This would have rendered his labour useless. Immediate fruit needs to be matured and well established. We desire that no aspect of our lives or ministries should be wasted.

Chuck Swindoll draws from this chapter seven ways to have a ministry which is valued and not in vain:

1. **The preaching is to be based on truth and not deceit (v.3)**
2. **The message is to be from God and not man (v.4)**
3. **The ministry is to be tender and not forceful (v.7))**
4. **The sharing is of the life and not just words (v.8)**
5. **The labour is because of dedication and not for reward or remuneration (vv.1,9)**
6. **The example is to be encouraging and not critical (vv.10,11)**
7. **The aim is to make godly men and women, not clones of oneself (v.12)**

The American paraphrase, 'The Message' renders 2 Thessalonians 2:16,17 in a way that expresses the desire of all true preachers of the word: 'May Jesus Himself and God our Father, who reached out in love and surprised you with gifts of unending help and confidence, put a fresh heart in you, and invigorate your work, enliven your speech.'

Verse 2

But even after we had suffered before and were spitefully treated at Philippi, as you know, we were bold in our God to speak to you the gospel of God in much conflict.

Persecution did not prevent Paul from preaching the gospel. Despite all that he had endured in Philippi, he continued boldly proclaiming the word of God. After all, men and women are going to hell unless they repent and believe. There are marching orders from our Captain, to go into all the world and preach the gospel to every creature, and as Napoleon said: 'No event ought to prevent a soldier from obeying.' So how dare we be deterred or distracted from the task? William MacDonald says: 'A less robust person would have thought of numerous theological reasons why God was calling him to some more congenial audiences, not Paul.' The injury and insults Paul and his fellow-workers had received in Philippi (see Acts 16:22-24) were the painful badges which demonstrated to all in Thessalonica that they were not religious con-men. Their bodies may have been scarred after their beating, but their spirits were not discouraged. Unswerving commitment to the task in hand, and love for the people they ministered to, were their credentials. By the grace of God, Paul was the man that he was.

All true Christian ministry has a three-fold backcloth:

- **historic Christian truth (1:10)—it is real**
- **present Christian conflict (2:2)—it is relevant**
- **future Christian certainty (1:10; 2:19)—it is reassuring**

The ministry therefore has a solid foundation of truth, and so it will have the effect of encouraging people and strengthening them in their hope.

The Christian gospel that 'Christ died for our sins, according to the Scriptures, and that He was buried, and that He rose again the third day, according to the Scriptures' is the most vital news in the world, and at all costs, it must be placarded to a watching world, shouted to a listening world and lived out to a world that rarely sees reality. The Lord deliberately 'made Himself of no reputation', for the reputation of the world is not a thing to be sought for. The Christian's body and being is to be made disposable to the will, work and ways of God. Anything less than that is refusing to accept his lordship. Believers have been bought with the precious blood of Christ, so their response to such love ought to be total surrender to and service for him.

> All my days and all my hours,
> All my will and all my powers,
> All the passion of my soul—
> Not a fragment, but the whole,
> Shall be Thine, dear Lord.

Verses 3–4

For our exhortation did not come from error or uncleanness, nor was it in deceit. But as we have been approved by God to be entrusted with the gospel, even so we speak, not as pleasing men, but God who tests our hearts.

Integrity is a key Christian quality. Paul exposed his motives to the people whose lives were transformed through his ministry, and who had suffered so much since believing. He was not guilty of deceit—he preached the truth of the gospel, even if it appeared unpalatable. There were no impure motives in his work, nor cunning treachery. The ministry is a sacred stewardship. God has entrusted each believer with the gospel (an oft-repeated word in this epistle), and nobody has any right to tamper with it.

Paul knew that God uses the person who uses the message that God uses! Ultimately, our judge is not other human beings, but God himself. Our hearts are continually laid bare before him. We shall one day appear before him. This is not a human court with biases, it is the judgment seat of Christ. Therefore, it will not be influenced by what our friends (who might speak in favour of us), or our enemies (who might speak against us) say, but we will be judged according to truth. Paul could say of himself, that the minister, the message, the ministry and motive were pure.

We should seek to follow the Lord Jesus who refused to negotiate truth, or adjust his message to please, in order to gather a larger crowd or have greater influence. He was hounded by his critics, mocked and sneered and jeered at, but he continued to speak boldly and live to fulfil his high purpose. Dare his disciples do anything less? We must refuse to be gagged by intimidators. As H. G. Wells said, 'The trouble with so many people is that the voice of their neighbours sounds louder in their ears than the voice of God.'

Daily meeting with God, and simply obeying what he says, will keep us straightforwardly preaching 'Christ and him crucified'. We should frequently ask whether we seek to please men or God.

Verse 5
For neither at any time did we use flattering words, as you know, nor a cloak for covetousness—God is witness.

Someone defined the difference between flattery and gossip as: 'Flattery is what we say to someone's face which we would never say behind their back', but 'Gossip is what we say behind some-one's back which we would never say to their face!' Flattery is telling people what they want to hear in order that they will do what you want them to do. That is not communication, it is manipulation. It shows a lack of sincerity and integrity. Paul, like his Lord before him, was not guilty of this. He preached the truth in love. The gospel does not flatter people. It honestly states our guilty position before God, but it does give significance to our life, in that, 'while we were still sinners Christ died for us' (Rom. 5:8), and indeed, as Christians, 'we are His workmanship created in Christ Jesus for good works . . .' (Eph. 2:10). This is his doing and it is (not, we are!) marvellous in our eyes.

Money and ministry have always appeared to clash. 'For every hundred who can handle failure, there's only one who can handle success', said George MacDonald. Every Christian is to be above reproach in the area of finance, for we are accountable to God. He is well able to provide all that we need, and at just the right moment. If riches increase, then we have the privilege of being good stewards and helping our brothers and sisters who are in less fortunate situations than ourselves.

Richard Baxter, the great Puritan said, 'Take heed to yourselves, lest your example contradict your doctrine, and lest you lay such stumbling blocks before the blind, as may be the occasion of their ruin; lest you unsay with your lives, what you say with your tongues; and be the greatest hinderers of success of our own labours.' It is 'a fearful thing' to be 'an unsanctified preacher'. We need to ask ourselves which is the more important—money or ministry?

For a number of years, Charles E. Fuller was the most 'successful' Christian radio broadcaster in the USA. He was spending $30,000 a week to air the 'Old Fashioned Revival Hour' on 465 stations across America. He was asked about his success and replied, 'I'm not interested in figures, I'm interested in souls. Some say I reach twenty million people. I don't know. All I know is that I preach the greatest message in the world. There may be greater orators, but nobody can preach a greater message, because I preach from the world's greatest Book. It is the old gospel, the simple gospel that pulls.' This world has no higher calling than that of being a proclaimer of the gospel.

Verses 6-7

Nor did we seek glory from men, either from you or from others, when we might have made demands as apostles of Christ. But we were gentle among you, just as a nursing mother cherishes her own children.

At the end of the 1983 Conference for Itinerant Evangelists, the 5,000 people present were asked to make solemn promises concerning their lives and ministries. One of the 'Amsterdam Affirmations', as they were called, read: 'We acknowledge our obligation, as servants of God, to lead lives of holiness and moral purity, knowing that we exemplify Christ to the church and the world', and we pledge ourselves to be 'faithful stewards of all that God gives us, and to be accountable to others in the finances of our ministry.'

Christians are to be different. Stories of Christians treating others with lack of love or respect ought not to be. Paul could say that he did not make unjustifiable demands on others, even though he was an apostle. We should follow his example. We have no right to make unwarranted demands. Because of their position, knowledge and abilities, abusing authority is a particularly powerful temptation for Christian leaders, but it is to be shunned by those who are truly seeking to minister. As a preacher of the gospel, I should strive as much to make my life consistent, as I do to prepare a sermon. I am to live to please the Lord, and not others.

Paul compares himself to a nurse, or a nursing mother. He treated the Christians with whom he was working with tender dignity and loving care. *How* a mother feeds her child is almost as important as *what* she feeds the little one with. Gentleness is showing personal care appropriate to another's emotional needs. Do you remember the Aesop fable of the driving wind and the scorching sun? The wind and the sun competed to get a man to take off his coat. The warmth of the sun won the day. As Christians, let us avoid the 'big stick' approach, turning aside from the temptation to vilify, criticise, and beat others into submission. We do not want to be known as crusty, but caring Christians!

In Ezekiel 16, God pictures himself as a loving parent to his people. Paul treats Christians with similar concern. It is said of John Wesley that he had no children of his own, but he had tens of thousands of spiritual children. We are to tenderly treat all those we have dealings with. 'Be kind, you do not know what battles people are fighting' were the words written in the fly leaf of the Bible of John Watson, the Scottish preacher. It is always a hurtful thing to see a parent being unkind to his or her physical children; how much worse to see people behaving badly toward their children in the faith.

Verses 8-9

So, affectionately longing for you, we were well pleased to impart to you not only the gospel of God, but also our own lives, because you had become dear to us. For you remember, brethren, our labour and toil; for labouring night and day, that we might not be a burden to any of you, we preached to you the gospel of God.

Every Christian feels a deep sense of gratitude to God for all that was accomplished in Christ's willing sacrifice on the cross. We love him because he first loved us and gave himself for us. To give our lives absolutely without reservation, as living sacrifices to him, is the finest way of expressing our deepest gratitude to God.

There have been many Christians throughout twenty centuries of church history who have given themselves to proclaim Christ. Their preaching of Christ, despite ignorance and opposition, is a challenge to us all. Satan would whisper that such a life is miserable and legalistic. That is far from the truth. In our century,

Gladys Aylward, after a life-time of missionary service in China said: 'I have not done what I wanted to; I have not eaten what I wanted or worn what I would have chosen; I have lived in houses that I would not have looked at twice; I longed for a husband and babies, and security and love, but God never gave them; instead He left me alone for 17 years with one book—a Chinese Bible. I don't know anything about the latest novels, pictures and theatres. I live in a rather out-dated world and I suppose you would say it is awful miserable isn't it? Friend, I have been one of the happiest women who stepped this earth. I have known the heavens opening and the blessing tumbling out.'

Paul loved the Thessalonians so much that he would have given his life for them. He refused the temptation to put up his feet, go for the easy option, and feed his own rights. People in Thessalonica were lost, dying and going to hell. Paul knew the only way of escape—Christ and him crucified. Whatever the personal cost to himself, he *had* to proclaim this message. The unsaved had to be saved, and then built up in the grace and knowledge of the Lord Jesus. No task was more important to Paul than this.

Paul worked as a tent-maker by day, to raise the funds to fulfil his calling as an evangelist and pastor. Therefore he worked both night and day. The Philippian believers gave gifts to help Paul in his evangelism in Thessalonica (see Phil. 4:16). Like a mother-to-be in travail, he laboured. It was productive pain, as he gave birth to spiritual children and saw them mature into fruitful Christians able to grow despite the 'stones' of persecution (Matt. 13:20-21) which lay all around them. Love for Christ, and for the lost was his motivation.

Sam Hadley had lived a deeply ungodly life before his remarkable conversion through the Water Street Mission in New York. He eventually became the superintendent of that rescue mission. Charles Alexander was the evangelist R. A. Torrey's song leader, but had been brought up in a carefully protected Christian home. It was suggested that Alexander should meet with Hadley to be shown the seedier side of life that so many were involved in, which Alexander had never seen. The two met and started their somewhat strange time together. Eventually, after visiting pubs and clubs and what used to be called 'dens of iniquities', Charles Alexander had had enough. He and Sam Hadley parted, but Alexander noticed that Hadley had stopped walking. Turning to look, he noticed in the shadows that Sam Hadley was leaning against the gas lamp. Thinking that he was perhaps feeling ill, Alexander walked up to Hadley and was about to ask how he was, when he heard the deep groans of a burdened man: 'Oh, the sin of this city; the sin of this city; the sin of this city is breaking my heart, Oh God!' Such deep emotion will be felt by all who are sincerely burdened for souls. This sense of burden grows as we are willing to be involved in the work of winning souls for Christ.

Verses 10-12

You are witnesses, and God also, how devoutly and justly and blamelessly we behaved ourselves among you who believe; as you know how we exhorted, and comforted, and charged every one of you, as a father does his own children, that you would walk worthy of God who calls you into His own kingdom and glory.

These verses bring to a climax how the pattern-saint Paul was able to describe his ministry among the Thessalonians. Chuck Swindoll says: 'The Apostle incarnated the gospel in the reality of his own life. He opened up his secrets, his struggles, his scars, his humanity —and he worked hard to live out the principles he was trying to teach.' His ministry showed boldness (v.2), was without deceit, uncleanness or guile (v.3), was pleasing to God and not men (v.4,6), was without flattery or covetousness (v.5), did not make unjustifiable demands on the hearers (v.6), and was characterized by gentleness, affection and commitment (v.7,8). Now in verses ten to twelve, Paul could testify to how devoutly, justly and blamelessly he and his friends behaved themselves when ministering. I wonder how many of these descriptive words describe our lives. For Paul, they derived from his inmost passion to 'walk worthy of God who calls us into His own kingdom and glory.' Surely, there can be no higher motivation. Paul often uses walking as a metaphor for the steady (if unspectacular) progress that should characterize the Christian. A walk is a repeated step. Day by day we are to make the right choices and so walk worthy of God, who has called us to be his.

Paul's aim in writing to the Thessalonian believers was to exhort (not extort!), comfort and charge (or implore) them. Having likened himself to a nursing mother in verse seven, he now compares himself to a father with his own children. The greatest model of a father is God. (Parents should act towards their children as God acts towards his.) He sets the pattern of true fatherhood, and Paul followed this with the Christians with whom he was involved. On the foundation of Christ, he constructed with bricks of truth, holiness and integrity, cemented together by love, a building which would be evident in the area around, and bring much glory to God. If the best sermon is that of a holy life, Paul was a great preacher.

Verse 13
For this reason we also thank God without ceasing, because when you received the word of God which you heard from us, you welcomed it not as the word of men, but as it is in truth, the word of God, which also effectively works in you who believe.

Paul, still wanting to hearten the Christians of Thessalonica, explains that he thanks God for them. They were not an embarrassment to him. Three times, Paul gives thanks for this church (see 1:2; 2:13; 3:9). They had 'received' or welcomed the word of God, discerning that what was proclaimed to them was not the word of man, but the word of God. F. F. Bruce in his *Word Biblical Commentary* on this epistle says, 'The word of human beings, however wise in substance or eloquent in expression, cannot produce spiritual life: this is the prerogative of the word of God.' So our responsibility is to faithfully pray and faithfully proclaim. God will then take and use his word to bring life where, as in Ezekiel's vision (Ezek. 37), there has been death and decay. 'Preaching is truth through personality', said Phillips Brooks. God uses people. What an awesome thought! The church in Thessalonica comprised converted Jews, God-fearing Jews and former idolatrous pagans. Though varied in background, each had come to Christ through the word being planted in their hearts.

Each believer has the responsibility to ensure that the word is what is being proclaimed, and that the temptation to dabble in new and fanciful notions is resisted. Such can be attractive for preachers of the word because they lead to the preacher being a focus of attention. Christ must increase, and we must decrease. We are to point people away from ourselves, and toward the Lord. This means at times that the Christian leader has actively to resist becoming a celebrity in the eyes of the Christian world. The church is Christ's church, not the church of a particular leader or pastor. God will not share his glory with any other, and may have to humble the Christian leader if that simple truth is forgotten.

Paul refused to charge people to hear the gospel (1 Cor. 9:18), and he refused to change his gospel for people. The main thing was that he made the main thing, the main thing! The result was that the Thessalonians appreciated, appropriated and applied the word of God to themselves. There are different ways of preaching the word, e.g. one might use Bible texts, another may develop themes, whilst yet another may systematically expound passages; but the principal objective is to preach the word of God. (*c.f.* the preaching styles of C. H. Spurgeon with Dr Martyn Lloyd-Jones, D. L. Moody with Harry Ironside—each preached the word, but in such different styles. Each was used by God for his own purposes.) There is still a hunger for spiritual reality in the hearts of some people today. It is a great encouragement for a preacher to have a congregation that is seriously intent on hearing, heeding and then heralding the word. Attendance upon, and attentiveness to, preaching by congregations is greatly encouraging to those who proclaim the word of God.

Verses 14-16

For you, brethren, became imitators of the churches of God which are in Judea in Christ Jesus. For you also suffered the same things from your own countrymen, just as they did from the Judeans, who killed both the Lord Jesus and their own prophets, and have persecuted us; and they do not please God and are contrary to all men, forbidding us to speak to the Gentiles that they may be saved, so as always to fill up the measure of their sins; but wrath has come upon them to the uttermost.

How much should we follow the example of other Christians? Only as far as they follow Christ. When John Robinson, the pastor of the congregation of refugee Puritans at Leiden in Holland was bidding farewell to the party of exiles leaving for New England on the *Mayflower*, he said: 'I charge you, that you follow me no farther that you have seen me follow the Lord Jesus Christ.' The Christians in Judea set an example worthy to be followed, and the Thessalonian Christians took up the challenge.

Have you ever wondered how you would cope if persecution towards believers came to your country? Of course, God gives grace for every situation, but one is filled with a sense of admiration for those in church history who have stood firm for Christ, despite the cost. Today in parts of the world, especially in Moslem lands, Christians endure much because of their faithfulness to Christ. This is nothing new, and throughout the New Testament we are warned of the consequences of living in a world which hated Christ and will hate his followers. In the West, persecution can come in the subtle form of pressure from educators, employers, social services and pressure groups.

What a privilege, though, to be able to suffer for the Lord Jesus who left the splendour of heaven and came to earth to suffer and die for you and me. Didn't Christ say that we should even rejoice and be glad when reviling and persecution come our way (Matt. 5:10-12; see also 1 Pet. 1:7)? To his persecuted children, God gives the promise of sufficient grace for every situation (2 Cor. 9:8) and the certainty that one day there will be the reward of not only salvation (Eph. 2:8-9), and a crown (Rev. 2:10); but for the persecutors, there will be wrath. Let us pray for these people, that they will be converted to Christ, before that great day of judgment.

Despite cynicism, criticism and opposition, we must not be silenced. Like Peter and John we must take the attitude: 'Whether it is right in the sight of God to listen to you more than to God, you judge. For we cannot but speak the things which we have seen and heard' (Acts 4:19,20). It is all too easy to grow to conform to, and even love, the world which persecuted and killed the Lord and so many of his followers.

We are commanded to pray for our enemies. Do we also pray for our brothers and sisters in various parts of the world who are, at this moment, being persecuted for righteousness sake (2 Tim. 1:16)? It may be that by so doing we will refresh them, and ourselves.

Verses 17-20

But we, brethren, having been taken away from you for a short time in presence, not in heart, endeavoured more eagerly to see your face with great desire. Therefore we wanted to come to you— even I, Paul, time and again—but Satan hindered us. For what is our hope, or joy, or crown of rejoicing? Is it not even you in the presence of our Lord Jesus Christ at His coming? For you are our glory and joy.

We all have desires, aims and ambitions; God either establishes or disposes of them. At times Paul was prevented from going somewhere by the Spirit; at other times it was Satan who hindered him. Paul was sufficiently in touch with God as to know who was hindering him. The word 'hindered' paints a picture of Satan going ahead cutting into the pathway of Paul, breaking up the road. The devil is our adversary, seeking to thwart the evangelization of the world. He is to be treated seriously and resisted. When the Spirit held Paul back, it was because the Lord had something better (and often bigger) for him. When Satan hindered him, it was a negative and destructive thing. The Lord over-rules all of Satan's strategies. If Paul had been able to visit the Thessalonians, we may not have had this letter. We need not fear that the devil is obstructing our way. If we walk with God, we will find that our steps and our stops are ordered by the Lord.

How Paul loved these Christians! They were his hope, joy, glory, and crown of rejoicing, and therefore he longed to see them. They were his brothers and sisters in Christ and very dear indeed to Paul. Paul, having been torn from the Thessalonians felt bereft of them, or as the Greek word implies, he felt orphaned by his separation from them. Chapter 2, like each of the other chapters in this little book, ends on the triumphant theme of Christ's second coming.

Can you imagine the sheer joy and bliss of being in heaven and meeting the Saviour with other believers? I do not want to be there empty handed, but with those whom I have had the privilege of winning to Christ. That will be a crown of glory, and I will want to cast it down at the throne saying, 'You are worthy, O Lord, to receive glory and honour and power . . .' (Rev. 4:10-11). It will be a thrill on that great judgment day to see saints who came to the Lord through our work and witness. That will be a cause for great rejoicing. (See Dan. 12:3; 2 Cor. 1:14 and Phil. 2:16).

Anne Ross Cousin turned into verse the thoughts of Samuel Rutherford (1600–60) as he lay in prison in Aberdeen thinking of his congregation in Anworth:

Fair Anworth on the Solway
To me thou still art dear;
Even from the verge of heaven
I drop for thee a tear.

O! if one soul from Anworth
Shall meet me at God's right hand,
My heaven shall be two heavens
In Immanuel's land.

At present, Christians the world over share in suffering. If persecution mounts and difficulties appear intolerable, let us be reminded that Christ is coming to this earth in glory and splendour. He is a friend of mine, and I will be with him for all eternity. He who will come, has come and does come to me when I call upon him.

Chapter four

A church matures

1 Thessalonians 3

Verse 1-5

Therefore, when we could no longer endure it, we thought it good to be left in Athens alone, and sent Timothy, our brother and minister of God, and our fellow labourer in the gospel of Christ, to establish you and encourage you concerning your faith, that no one should be shaken by these afflictions; for you yourselves know that we are appointed to this. For, in fact, we told you before when we were with you that we would suffer tribulation, just as it happened, and you know. For this reason, when I could no longer endure it, I sent to know your faith, lest by some means the tempter had tempted you, and our labour might be in vain.

Having seen how the church was born (chap.1), and nurtured (chap. 2), we now see how it was established (chap.3). Warren Wiersbe has shown how Paul used various means to establish the believers: he sent a helper (vv.1-2), he wrote them a letter (vv.11-13). Here is a model of how Christ establishes us as Christians today.

The pioneer missionary, C. T. Studd, said, 'Mere soul saving is easy—what is difficult is making those converts into soldiers, saints and soul-winners!' Paul was not content to have statistics of people being converted, but he desired and therefore prayed that the Thessalonian Christians would grow in faith, hope and love. 'Faith' is found in verses 2, 5, 6, 7 and 10 in chapter 3, and 'love' is mentioned in verses 6 and 12, but there is no mention of hope. The believers had not lost hope (see 1:3), but Paul was concerned that it should not be destroyed under the pressure of persecution (see v.5). Seeking to stir up hope, he reminds the Christians of the second coming of Christ. Their afflictions had been predicted and were to be expected, and should not therefore have discouraged these disciples of the Lord.

God, as a loving heavenly Father, allows us to go through trials to refine us, not for us to redefine our understanding of him. Trials accomplish much in our lives. They serve to:

◆ prove the reality of our faith (see 1 Pet. 1:7)
◆ enable us to comfort others (see 2 Cor. 1:4)
◆ develop graces within us (see Rom. 5:3)
◆ stir up zeal in evangelism (see Acts 4:29)
◆ remove the dross from our lives (see Job 23:10)

Warren Wiersbe says, 'Faith that cannot be tested cannot be trusted.' Tests do not destroy faith, they develop it. Suffering and faith in Christ are inseparable. God uses the difficulties we face to refine us and make us more like Christ. Whatever we are called to go through, God keeps his eye on the clock and the temperature gauge—he knows how long and how hot is right for us.

A thing may not necessarily be God's commanded will, but if it happens to us it is in God's will for us. God is able to take the worst of scenarios and make them work for good. It is worth remembering that God uses for his glory those people and things that are broken: God broke Jacob at Peniel before clothing him with spiritual power (Gen. 32:22-32); Gideon's 300 men broke their pitchers and defeat came to the adversaries (Judg. 7:19-25); Mary broke her alabaster box and the perfume gave a sweet aroma to the whole house (Matt. 26:6-13); Jesus broke the five loaves and two fishes and fed 5,000 men (John 6:1-14); Jesus' body was bro-

44

ken by the thorns, nails and spear, but redemption poured from him to sinful men and women the world over (Matt. 26:26). All God's intentions towards his children are loving, and every situation is used for our good and his glory (Rom. 5:3; 8:28). F. B. Meyer in his *Our Daily Homily* expresses this truth well: 'The sweetest scents are only obtained by tremendous pressure; the fairest flowers grow amid Alpine snow-solitudes, the rarest gems have suffered longest from the lapidary's wheel; the noblest statues have borne most blows of the chisel.'

Paul could not wash his hands of the believers in Thessalonica. He genuinely liked and loved them. Paul was aware that Satan is the enemy of souls, and he was not ignorant of his sinister devices. Concerned for them, he sent his trusted and esteemed 'son in the faith' Timothy to encourage and establish them. Oh, to be so reliable and dependable, a useful vessel for the Master, thoroughly equipped and prepared for every good work! How thrilled Paul would have been when he heard that his labour had not been in vain.

John Sung, the Chinese evangelist, used to keep scrap books filled with photos and information about those who had been converted through his ministry. He sought to work faithfully through these, praying for them on a regular basis. Could it be that the Lord would trust us to win people to Christ, if we could be trusted to diligently follow them up afterwards?

Verses 6-10
But now that Timothy has come to us from you, and brought us good news of your faith and love, and that you always have good remembrance of us, greatly desiring to see us, as we also to see you—therefore, brethren, in all our affliction and distress we were comforted concerning you by your faith. For now we live, if you stand fast in the Lord. For what thanks can we render to God for you, for all the joy with which we rejoice for your sake before our God, night and day praying exceedingly that we may see your face and perfect

45

what is lacking in your faith?

Timothy could reassure Paul of the steadfastness of the believers in Thessalonica, because of what he saw in their lives. I have heard it said that it is easier to weep when others weep than it is to rejoice when others rejoice. Paul was a bigger man than that, and he rejoiced with other people's rejoicing, even though he was in distress. When things are not well with us individually, the blessings which others are enjoying can be means of encouraging us. Paul was afflicted and distressed, but comforted by the spiritual progress of the church.

Genuine joy was found in the heart of Paul. His habit was to pray for the believers in Thessalonica, that their:

- **faith would mature (v.10)**
- **love would abound (v.12)**
- **hope would transform them (v.13)**

Every Christian can and should be involved in the ministry of prayer for others. The story is told of a servant-girl who was asked what Christian work she did. She said that her responsibilities were such that time was limited as far as activity was concerned, but she said, 'When I go to bed I take the morning newspapers with me, and I read the notices of the births and I pray for the babies; and I read the notices of marriage and I pray that those who have been married will be happy; and I read the announcements of death and I pray that the sorrowing may be comforted.' Who knows what blessing resulted from the faithful, intelligent praying of that girl?

Paul wanted to meet the church again. Their chatter would not have been inconsequential. He wanted to invest in their lives and be of lasting, spiritual benefit to them. I recall many conversations over the years which have been significant. Memorable moments are made when someone who is walking with the Lord shares his or her insights in a way that touches the nerves and needs of our lives at that time.

Verse 10
Night and day praying exceedingly that we may see your face and perfect what is lacking in your faith?

Paul says to the Thessalonians that he is concerned to 'perfect what is lacking in your faith'. What exactly does that mean? The Greek word for 'lacking' has rich meaning and varied usage. It means to fit together, to join, to restore, to repair or to equip. It is used of reconciling political differences; it is a surgical term for 'setting bones'; it describes the repairing of nets (e.g. Mark 1:19), and it is used of making military and naval preparations. It is as if Paul is acting as a doctor applying healing balm to people's souls, or a fisherman mending the broken twine of belief, or a military commander instructing the believers to do battle with Satan.

Here are some characteristics of true faith:

- ◆ it is restful (Heb. 4:3). The soul can be satisfied in its secure relationship with the Lord.
- ◆ it is joyful (1 Pet. 1:8). How glad we are that Jesus is our Lord, Saviour, Friend and King.
- ◆ it is hopeful (Heb. 11:1; Gal. 5:5). Our faith teaches us that whilst we are blessed at present, the best is yet to come.
- ◆ it is loving (Gal. 5:6; Eph. 6:23). Christian qualities complement and encourage each other—faith will build up love.
- ◆ it is practical (Jas. 2:20). True faith, which is inward, will show itself outwardly.
- ◆ it is patient (2 Tim. 3:10. Heb. 6:11; Rev. 13:10). Faith is

confident that God is the perfect time-keeper.
- ◆ it is victorious (1 John 5:4). Christ is the Victor. Faith reminds the soul of that truth.
- ◆ it is vocal (2 Cor. 4:13). Faith speaks, and speaking strengthens faith.
- ◆ it is ever-growing (2 Cor. 10:15; 2 Thess. 1:3). Exercising faith leads to it becoming stronger.

Faith is not a leap in the dark, or even a gushy feeling; it rests on the solid promises of God, and then acts on them. Acts of obedience to the word of God are acts of faith. Do you want more faith? Read, and then obey the Word of God, and watch your faith grow.

Verses 11-13
Now may our God and Father Himself, and our Lord Jesus Christ, direct our way to you. And may the Lord make you increase and abound in love to one another and to all, just as we do to you, so that He may establish your hearts blameless in holiness before our God and Father at the coming of our Lord Jesus Christ with all His saints.

Paul prays that both the Father and the Lord Jesus may enable him to visit them. He also prays that in his absence the Thessalonian believers may love each other more and more. It is a totally selfless prayer, devoid of vain repetition, but relevant to the specific needs of the Thessalonians. Scanning a shopping list was not Paul's way of praying, and he was not ashamed to repeatedly bring before the Lord the major concerns of his heart.

There are three key ideas in these verses: holiness, love, and coming. Paul will develop these in the next chapter—holiness (4:1-8), love (4:9-10), and Christ's coming (4:13-18). The pattern is clear—before teaching, Paul prayed. His letter was not merely space filling. He was 'scratching where the Thessalonians were itching', and also seeking to make them itch in the right places! By praying and then teaching, Paul was making the maximum impact on the church which he loved. Prayer and blessing have been married, and no one can put asunder what God has joined together.

The Thessalonian Christians loved one another. They set an example for all Christians, for all time. The great American evangelist, D. L. Moody said: 'Strife is Satan's strategy. There is one thing I have noticed as I have travelled in different countries: I have never known the Spirit of the Lord to work where the people are divided. There is one thing that we must have if we are to have the Holy Spirit of God work in our midst, and that is unity.'

Faith, love and hope grow by being exercised—use them or lose them. Similarly, the ability to pray grows through regular usage. I believe there are fewer real pray-ers than we imagine, but more than we sometimes fear. Are you one? We need to pray intelligently for each other. Our prayers should be well-informed. God commands us to pray. Experience proves the value of time spent praying. All the great saints of Scripture and history have been men and women of prayer. Therefore, let us pray!

And in praying, we are preparing ourselves to meet him. On that day, we want him to be a friend whom we know, not a stranger whom we have to get to know!

Chapter five

A church encouraged

1 Thessalonians 4

Chapters 4 and 5 of 1 Thessalonians contain the practical applications of all that Paul has been re-stating in the first three chapters of the book. In chapter 2:12 we read of walking worthy of God. That theme is now developed:

- **walk in holiness (4:1-8)**
- **walk in love (4:9-10**
- **walk honestly (4:11,12)**
- **walk in hope (4:13-18)**
- **walk in light (5:1-11)**
- **walk in gratitude (5:12-13)**
- **walk in obedience (5:14-28)**

However, it is important that we remember that this epistle is primarily one of encouragement. Derek Bingham wrote a book entitled, *Don't wait until he's dead*. The thrust was that we should encourage people while they are alive, not just speaking nicely about them when they have died. It is a good thing to seek to encourage people in what they are doing for the Lord. Paul is genuine in his desire to cheer and encourage the believers in a difficult situation. He really did feel thankful to God for who they were and all that had been accomplished in them so far. However, he also wanted them to learn, and grow, in order that they might be moving towards excellence and Christ-likeness.

Verses 1-2
Finally then, brethren, we urge and exhort in the Lord Jesus that you should abound more and more, just as you received from us how you ought to walk and to please God; for you know what commandments we gave you through the Lord Jesus.

Do you remember your first step of faith? Has that now become a walk of faith? Walking with God is pleasing to God. Scripture teaches that I am to walk worthy:

- ◆ of my calling (Eph. 4:1)
- ◆ of the gospel (Phil. 1:27)
- ◆ of God (1 Thess. 2:12)

Everybody lives to please somebody (see 2:4). As Christians we want to follow the example of Enoch (see Heb. 11:5), who walked with God, or even more that of the Lord Jesus (see John 8:29), who consistently delighted to do the will of his Father.

'If it feels good, do it' has become the philosophy of the age. It is easy for this nobody's-right-or-wrong notion to affect the church. Christianity is not a legalistic list of dos and don'ts, but there are absolutes. God gave the Ten Commandments (written in Exod. 20), and Paul here speaks of the 'commandments we gave you through the Lord Jesus'. Ours is a sex-crazed society, and the spirit of the age is completely foreign to the Holy Spirit who lives and works in the believer. Christians are the very dwelling place of God, and therefore we are to yield our bodies to him.

Am I a holy person? Do I desire to be holy so that I might 'see' the Lord. Am I passionate about being pure? Do I flirt with the opposite sex? Is my conversation consistent with being a follower of the Lord Jesus Christ? Am I claiming the promise of 1 John 1:9 and confessing my sin, and finding him faithful and just to forgive my sin and to cleanse me from all unrighteousness? Thankfully the Lord is willing and able to create in me a clean heart, when I turn from sin and trust the Saviour. (See Proverbs 28:13.)

Verses 3-5

For this is the will of God, your sanctification: that you should abstain from sexual immorality; that each of you should know how to possess his own vessel in sanctification and honour, not in passion of lust, like the Gentiles who do not know God;

Have you ever wondered what is the will of God for your life? One thing is certain, he desires to see you sanctified—set apart for his service. Specifically, Paul applies this to include abstinence from sexual immorality. Sex is not wrong. When God created the first man and woman, he created them with a sexual drive, yet he still pronounced his creation 'very good'. Sex within the security and commitment of marriage is right and proper (see Heb. 13:4). It is a God-given means of protecting one's spouse from the temptations of immorality (1 Cor. 7:2). Sex outside of marriage, in any form, is always sin. There are no exceptions to this. Faithfulness in marriage is an outworking of faithfulness in our walk with God. We have become all too familiar with tragic stories of 'great' people falling into sin. Such disasters start with the neglecting of secret prayer, then tolerating the possibility of sin, and finally being lured into it.

Bishop J. C. Ryle said, we 'must not expect sin, excite sin, or excuse sin'. In his letter James likens sin to the cycle of human life: 'When desire has conceived, it gives birth to sin; and sin when it is full-grown, brings forth death' (Jas. 1:15). Very quickly, the thought can become an act, but the Bible is firm: 'Adulterers and

53

adulteresses! Do you not know that friendship with the world is enmity with God. Whoever therefore wants to be a friend of the world makes himself an enemy of God' (Jas.4:-4).

To guard against sin sneaking into the citadel of our hearts, we must wage war against sin in our lives (*cf.* 1 Pet. 2:11). We must ask the Lord to enable us to renounce all that is wrong and live whole-heartedly for him. This commitment will affect such areas of our lives as our television-viewing habits, the magazines and newspapers we look at, the things we own, the places we go, and the people with whom we get involved. Without condemning those with different standards, we will want to have the highest that we might please him who has chosen us to be his soldiers.

Learning to 'possess' one's own vessel surely refers to disciplining ourselves, by avoiding lust and pursuing holiness. Lust is deadly. Let me illustrate with a grisly example. Do you know how an Eskimo kills a wolf? First, the Eskimo coats his knife blade with animal blood and allows it to freeze. Then he adds layer upon layer of blood. Next, the hunter fixes his knife in the ground with its blade facing up. When the wolf with his sensitive nose smells the scent of blood, he begins to lick faster and faster, more vigorously lapping the blade until the keen edge is bare. The licking becomes feverish and his craving leads to him not noticing the razor-sharp sting of the naked blade on his own tongue, nor does he recognize that his insatiable thirst is being satisfied by his own blood. Shortly, the wolf lays dead in the snow.

Lust has a similar impact. It is a fearful thing that people can be consumed by their own lusts. Scripture teaches that we are to cast 'down arguments and every high thing that exalts itself against the knowledge of God, bringing every thought into captivity to the obedience of Christ' (2 Cor. 10:5). In other words the battle against lust is won or lost in the thought-life of the believer.

The Christian will want to keep his or her body in sanctification and honour, knowing that we are fearfully and wonderfully made by God, who has bought us at the price of the precious blood of Christ. God is our Creator and Redeemer. The Christian's body has become the very dwelling place of God (1 Cor. 6:19), and is destined for resurrection. Until that day, we want to be 'a vessel unto honour, sanctified, and meet for the master's use' (2 Tim. 2:21 AV).

How do we overcome lust? First, by marriage, if possible (1 Cor. 7:1-2), and therefore by meeting each other's (sexual) needs. Secondly, by filling our minds with the things of God's Word and work (Psalm 119:9,11). Thirdly, by positively turning from the things of the world, to the person of Christ, refusing to give in to the lusts of the flesh (1 John 2:15-17). Every little action of the common day makes or unmakes character and godliness. Frederick Buechner, in his book, *Wishful thinking: a theological ABC*, defined lust as, 'the craving for salt, in a man who is dying of thirst.' Lust is the exact opposite of the word by word description of love in 1 Corinthians 13. Either love or lust will win the day in our hearts.

Verses 6-8

That no one should take advantage of and defraud his brother in this matter, because the Lord is the avenger of all such, as we also fore-warned you and testified. For God did not call us to uncleanness, but in holiness. Therefore he who rejects this does not reject man, but God, who has also given us His Holy Spirit.

There are marital blessings and obligations which protect our spouse from the devastating potential of falling into immorality. Defrauding a husband or a wife sexually is forbidden in Scripture (see 1 Cor. 7:5). Not only is it true that 'the Lord is the avenger of such', but Satan is often the exploiter of such situations as well. Beware! God has called us to holy living. Sexual intercourse within a marriage relationship is the means of expressing, consummating and deepening mutual love between the husband and wife. It is like a barometer of the relationship, revealing the state of each aspect of marriage.

'Defraud' may be applied more generally, too. Christians are not to take what is not theirs. To seek sexual gratification from anyone other than one's husband or wife is wrong. Defrauding can apply to an unmarried couple who are going further in their physical involvement than they should, flirtation with someone else's husband or wife, or behaving in such a way as to bring dishonour to one's body. Such behaviour is forbidden, because it dishonours the Lord, and our brothers and sisters in Christ. As if to reinforce the vital nature of this teaching, we are warned of God's vengeance against all such sins.

We who are called to be sanctified (vv.3,4) and holy (v.7), can choose to be holy (Rom. 6:19) and are challenged to be holy (1 Pet. 1:14-16). Holiness requires change (2 Cor. 5:17), and reveals true character (Eph. 5:8). Robert Murray McCheyne, the nineteenth century pastor from Dundee in Scotland, said, 'We are as holy as we choose to be.' Deciding our level of Christian commitment is our daily choice. Let us remember that to reject holiness is to reject God himself.

This teaching on sexuality is God's word, not man's ideas (v.8). Notice in verses 2, 3 and 8 that the three Persons of the Holy Trinity, Father, Son and Holy Spirit are concerned for our holiness, for God is holy. The NIV translates verse 8: '. . . God, who gives you his Holy Spirit'—this is present continuous. Upon conversion, the individual is filled, baptized with the Holy Spirit, but as a Black preacher put it, 'I leak!' We need continuous washing from sins and stains, and constant filling anew with God's Holy Spirit. If we ask, God will answer and give (see Luke 11:13).

Do you find it strange that Paul, in seeking to encourage these young, persecuted Christians, should spend valuable time writing of the delicacies of marriage? No, if we are walking with the Lord, *every* area of our life and relationships will be affected. There can be great joy in the fellowship of a marriage partnership which God can use to compensate for some of the pressures of daily Christian living. Now is a good time to review whether I am a good husband, or wife, or member of a family.

Verse 9

But concerning brotherly love you have no need that I should write to you, for you yourselves are taught by God to love one another;

True wisdom comes through knowing God and keeping his word. When we open the Scriptures and begin to read, we are opening the lips of God, and have the privilege of listening to him speak directly to us. God is concerned about the love of one Christian towards another.

How many churches do you know of which it could be said: 'But concerning brotherly love you have no need that I should write to you'? But the next part of the verse tells us how this could be true of us: 'for you yourselves are taught by God to love one another'. God has demonstrated his love toward us in that while we were yet sinners, Christ died for us. Our very existence is due to the love and mercy of God. He has loved us with an everlasting love. He has repeatedly commanded us to love one another. The badge of true Christianity is not how much we know, what books we have read or preachers we have heard, or where we have been and what we are involved in, but whether we love our brothers and sisters in Christ.

Vance Havner said, 'It was said of the early Christians, "How these Christians love each other!" Today the world might sometimes be more inclined to say, "How those Christians hate each other!". We have left our love for Christ, and when love for Christ dies, love for each other, for the Bible, for souls, dies.' These are challenging thoughts indeed! But situations can be changed, and practical Christian love can grow and become evident.

Love for our Christian brothers and sisters will demonstrate itself by a genuine interest in who they are and what they are doing. We may not agree with them wholly but as people who, like us, have recognized their need for salvation and have trusted Christ, surely we should love them. We will enquire of their well-being, pray for them, rejoice in their blessings, feel for them when times are tough; we will speak well of them, hold no grudges and value their fellowship and contribution in the service of the Lord. True love towards my brothers and sisters in Christ will be shown in a practical way.

Verses 10-12

And indeed you do so toward all the brethren who are in all Macedonia. But we urge you, brethren, that you increase more and more; that you also aspire to lead a quiet life, to mind your own business, and to work with your own hands, as we commanded you, that you may walk properly toward those who are outside, and that you may lack nothing.

The love of the Thessalonian Christians was not insular. Their love for the Lord led them to love each other as their brothers and sisters in the Lord. One of the great advantages in living in our day and age is that we can be well informed as to the state of the church beyond our immediate locality. What a privilege it is to keep in touch with, pray for, and give to people living or serving the Lord elsewhere. Missionary magazines and letters provide an excellent source of information that should not only fill our minds, but bend our knees in a genuine expression of unity in all that is being accomplished in the name of Christ. The church world-wide is a wonderful family, and we have much for which to be thankful to God.

Notice the holy discontent of Paul. He knew of the love of the church, but he urges that this might grow more and more. Paul wants the very best for himself and for others—the utmost for the Highest. The Christian will aspire for more—more of God, more of love, more of holiness, more to be able to give to others. The hymn, 'More about Jesus would I know' expresses this desire. I must not allow myself to become satisfied with my own spiritual state. 'As the deer pants for the water brooks so pants my soul for You, O God. My soul thirsts for God, for the living God' (Ps. 42:1-2).

What a contrast there is in this chapter! On the one hand there is lust (vv.1-8), and now there is love. Lust wants to get; love wants to give. Lust seeks to gratify itself; love wants to satisfy the needs of others. Lust destroys; love enlivens. Am I known as someone who genuinely loves people?

The church is enriched by people with differing temperaments and personalities. When a person is converted, God begins the process of changing the newly saved individual into Christ-likeness. 'We all . . . are being transformed into the same image from glory to glory, just as by the Spirit of the Lord' (2 Cor. 3:18). God chips away, refining and making us into the people we were meant to be. But whether extrovert or introvert, we are to avoid unnecessary controversy. We are to be the world's proclaimers, not the world's protesters. We are not to be dabbling in the affairs of others. An outline of what Jesus said to the disciples on the resurrection appearance by the lakeside (John 21) could be: catch fish, feed sheep, and mind your own business! (John 21:22). 'What is that to you?', is the question Jesus asked Peter—it could well be indelibly written over many a conversation, or etched on each telephone.

Paul then turned his attention to the issue of employment. Perhaps there were some in Thessalonica who were so much looking forward to the Lord's return that they could not see the point of secular work. This is hardly the Christian attitude. The Bible teaches that if we can be, we should be employed, not just standing around idly. God has given us skills and abilities, and we should use them all for his glory. Antonio Stradivari, the great maker of violins, said: 'If my hand slacked, I should rob God.' That is a good motto for us all. If unemployment has come our way, perhaps we could approach our church leadership and ask for suggestions as how we might profitably use our time in the service of the Lord. Become a valuable volunteer, until paid employment comes your way.

There is a watching world scrutinizing our every action and reaction. As Chuck Swindoll says:

They are watching and wondering, so conduct yourself with wisdom. They are listening and learning, so speak your words with grace. They are individuals and important, so respond with dignity and sensitivity.

Whatever we do, we should do heartily out of love for the Lord, not just for our employer. We are to work for the glory of God. (See Colossians 3:23.) A builder may construct a beautiful house for a wealthy client, but if he was to build one for his daughter and son-in-law to live in he would carefully and lovingly try to make everything the best. All our work is primarily for the Lord whom we love. In daily dependence upon God we are challenged in chapter 4:1-12, to lead holy, harmonious and honest lives. Verse 12 brings the teaching to a climax and conclusion. God has given us, and our church family, the means to provide for ourselves and our dependants. We will not lack if we use our talents and gifts for God's glory. 'No good thing will He withhold from those who walk uprightly.' (Ps. 84:11).

Verse 13
But I do not want you to be ignorant, brethren, concerning those who have fallen asleep, lest you sorrow as others who have no hope.

I can imagine scholars in Old Testament times debating from where the Messiah would come. I'm sure there would have been disagreements, as different ones emphasized and quoted one prophet or another. One group would say that he would come from Bethlehem, another would argue that Nazareth would be the place of his origin, and yet another maintain that he would emerge from Egypt. All had good authority for saying what they did. God wonderfully tied all the prophecies together, so that Christ was born in Bethlehem, fled as a baby to Egypt and grew up in Nazareth.

People have disagreed about the details of Christ's second coming. Don't be put off. There is wonderfully encouraging truth in this great theme. The vital thing is that Christ is coming again. Verse 13 teaches that there is therefore no need to be ignorant or sorrowful. We are to look forward to the moment of his return and to live in anticipation of it.

Such anticipation will affect our attitude to those whom we knew and loved, but who have died and gone to be with the Lord. They are better off, but we miss them. Yet we need not sorrow as do others who have no hope. It is not wrong to sorrow when we are bereft of a loved one. Even Jesus wept when he heard of the death of Lazarus. Tears which flow from a heart of love are natural. When you love deeply, you make yourself vulnerable. That is why, when a loved one is taken, the suffering is so severe. But, we need not sorrow as others sorrow when we know that the dear one is with the Lord, as it is only the body of the departed loved one that lies in the grave, the real person is with the Lord. On the tomb in South Africa, of the founder of the Scout movement, Lord Baden Powell are the words: 'I am not here; only my body is.' One day we will be with them, they with us, and together we will be with the Lord. What a day of rejoicing that will be! This in itself, is sufficient reason to be eagerly anticipating the return of the Lord Jesus Christ. 'Even so, come Lord Jesus, come!'

Verse 14

For if we believe that Jesus died and rose again, even so God will bring with Him those who sleep in Jesus.

Which is the more important, the death of Christ on the cross for us, or his resurrection?

The question is unanswerable. Without Christ's death there could have been no resurrection and without his resurrection we would not have the certainty that God had accepted the sacrifice of his

Son for us. As Paul says in this verse, we do believe that Jesus died. The cross on which Christ was crucified had four points, so let us consider four ideas about it:

- He *laid* on the cross. He who laid the foundations of the earth; who once lay in the virgin womb of his mother; who lay in the hinder part of a boat on the Sea of Galilee, and lay prostrate in the Garden of Gethsemane, lay naked on the cross of Calvary.

- He *stayed* on the cross. He could have called twelve legions of angels to rescue him, but he stayed there until he had fully paid the price of sin.

- He *paid* on the cross. Every last sin of mine and yours was carried by Christ as he paid the punishment it would take me all eternity to pay. He loved me and gave himself for me.

- He *prayed* on the cross. Christ prayed for the Roman soldiers who hurt him so much, and in so doing, he prayed for all of us who 'do not know what we do'.

Such amazing love, should surely win my heart and life.

Christians who have died are described as having 'fallen asleep'. They are said to sleep, not because they are unconscious, but because their decease was as devoid of terror as a little child's deep slumber. The apostle Paul prefers not to major on death, but instead speaks of 'departure', 'absent from the body', 'sleep', the dismantling of this 'earthly tabernacle', or 'to be with Christ'. When he does speak of death, he says, 'To die is gain' (Phil. 1:21).

Between the death and resurrection of Christ were hours when Christ lay cold and still in the tomb. His body was not decaying (Ps. 16:10). The angels of heaven must have been filled with a sense of wonder as the Lord of all glory lay wrapped in embalming cloths, buried in a tomb which had never been used before. The stone, the seal, and the soldiers were all in place to ensure that the body of Jesus would lie undisturbed, but someone had forgotten Old Testament prophecies and Jesus' own words, as well as the power of God. Christ tasted death for us all. His death was awful, but his rising again was to transcend all the horrors and traumas of Calvary.

Whatever has been assembled by the world's system will prove to be impotent when Christ returns in glory. The plans and purposes of God cannot be thwarted by the puny devices of mere mortals. All the powers of sin, death, Satan and hell were defeated when Christ rose from the tomb, leaving it empty of the one person it was designed to hold.

Death is one of Satan's great weapons. But Christ triumphed over it. He has paid for sin. He has conquered death. He was forsaken by God so that we might be forgiven and never be forsaken by him, in life, in death or in eternity. Hallelujah! We need not fear those who can destroy the body, but rather him who can destroy both body and soul in hell (Matt. 10:28).

Bask in the thought that Christ came, lived, died, was buried and rose again from the dead. Revel in the truth that Jesus is alive. The stone was rolled away from the tomb where Jesus lay, not so much to let Christ out, but to let us look in to the tomb and see that it is empty. Over the next few weeks Christ physically appeared to all types of people:

- ◆ the devoted—the women
- ◆ the discipled—the eleven remaining disciples
- ◆ the disappointed—Cleopas and the other on the road to Emmaus
- ◆ the doubting—Thomas
- ◆ the one who denied—Peter
- ◆ the dispersed—the 500 who saw the risen Jesus
- ◆ the disbeliever—Saul of Tarsus.

63

Whoever you are, whatever your past, wherever you have been, whatever you have done, you may meet with the conquering Christ. He has defeated sin and death and hell by rising again.

As certain as it is that Christ died and rose again, we know that Jesus will return to this earth, bringing with him all those who have loved him but have died before his return.

Verses 15-18

For this we say to you by the word of the Lord, that we who are alive and remain until the coming of the Lord will by no means precede those who are asleep. For the Lord Himself will descend from heaven with a shout, with the voice of an archangel, and with the trumpet of God. And the dead in Christ will rise first. Then we who are alive and remain shall be caught up together with them in the clouds to meet the Lord in the air. And thus we shall always be with the Lord. Therefore comfort one another with these words.

Christ's second coming to this earth will be a momentous event. For the believer it should be a doctrine that comforts (v.18) rather than a matter of controversy. The passage includes three basic comforts:

- **that death for the believer is sleep (v.14)**
- **that there will be a heavenly reunion (v.17)**
- **that there will be eternal blessing (v.17)**

Christ will return to this earth with the trumpet sound, a shout and the voice of an archangel. What a sound! Living Christians who are still remaining at the time of Christ's return will rise to meet the Lord in the air. He will bring with him those believers who have died before his return. In meeting Christ these will precede the living believers who will be caught up in the clouds to meet the Lord in the air. We shall reign with Christ and be with him forever, never to be separated. Christ will be acknowledged in his rightful position as King of kings and Lord of lords.

We do not know the day nor the hour of his return. Many Christians who are familiar with the signs which are to be fulfilled before his return, believe Christ's second coming will not be long delayed. The day of the Lord is at hand. This is a time to eagerly look forward to. What an incentive to live whole-heartedly for Christ now, 'while it is still day'. Regarding the second coming of Christ, there is a sound to hear, a sight to see, a miracle to feel, a meeting to enjoy and a comfort to experience. Will Christ's return be an embarrassing intrusion or a glorious climax to life for me? I remember hearing a missionary doctor from my own locality, Brian Wrigglesworth, who gave his life serving the Lord in South America, singing:

> And when He comes in bright array
> It will be glory then to say
> That 'He's a Friend of mine'.

The second coming of Christ is not only to be believed in the head, but its truth will affect the way I live in a very practical manner. If every sign is saying that the day of the Lord is drawing near, then this should lead me to:

- purify my life (1 Thess. 5:23; 1 John 3:3)
- evangelize the lost (Gen. 19:14)
- persevere (Rom. 8:18; 2 Cor. 4:17; 1 Thess. 4:18)
- maintain good relationships (Matt. 5:23; Js. 5:16)
- serve diligently (John 9:4)
- have an attitude of expectancy (Luke 12:36)
- keep abiding (1 John 2:28)

Great God, in whom we live,
Prepare us for that day;
Help us in Jesus to believe,
To watch, and wait, and pray.

Are you ready for the second coming of Christ?

Chapter six

A church strengthened

1 Thessalonians 5

We discover in the Bible and through experience that Christ both unites and divides (see John 7:43; 9:16; 10:19). In the first six verses of chapter five we find mentioned 'they' (twice) and 'you', 'us' or 'we' (six times). God does not see the world according to the economic situation, colour of skin, or sex, but as to whether an individual is trusting in Christ alone for salvation. The unsaved will be taken by surprise by the return of Christ for they will be unprepared for him. The Bible teaches that unbelievers are in the dark:

- ◆ their understanding is darkened (Eph. 4:18; 5:8)
- ◆ they love darkness (John 3:19–21)
- ◆ they are controlled by the power of darkness (Eph. 6:12)
- ◆ they are headed for eternal darkness (Matt. 8:12)

Christ will come as 'a thief in the night' to surprise the unconverted. We, as children of the light, ought not to be caught unawares; we should be looking for the signs of his return. When we have been on the Christian road for some years, it is hard to recall the darkness of being outside of Christ. If we can remember how we were, do we pity those who are still unsaved?

There will be great trouble in the world before his coming. It will be like a pregnant woman who is in labour before giving birth to her child. Of course, she does not look forward to the travail, but eagerly awaits the coming of the child. The birth pains are the indication that the child is near to being delivered. We do not look forward to troubles in the world, but as we look at them we know that Christ's second coming is drawing near. We should not despair when we see people who do evil, but we should confidently trust in the Lord (Ps. 37:1). There is coming a day when the lion will lie down with the lamb, and swords will be beaten into ploughshares, and people will learn war no more (Isa. 2:4).

Verses 1–4

But concerning the times and the seasons, brethren, you have no need that I should write to you. For you yourselves know perfectly that the day of the Lord so comes as a thief in the night. For when they say, 'Peace and safety!' then sudden destruction comes upon them, as labour pains upon a pregnant woman. And they shall not escape. But you, brethren, are not in darkness, so that this Day should overtake you as a thief.

Burglary seems to be an increasing problem of our society. One thing is sure, thieves do not give any warning of their coming. They take the owner of the house by surprise, as their appearance is unexpected and sudden. This is how the Lord's return will be to the unprepared and unsaved people of the earth.

The Bible speaks of the 'day of the Lord'. It is a time of judgment, desolation and darkness. On that day the proud and lofty will be brought low (Isa. 2:12). It will be a terrible day for many, and we must warn them: 'Blow the trumpet in Zion, and sound an alarm in My holy mountain! Let all the inhabitants of the land tremble, for the day of the Lord is coming for it is at hand . . .' (see Joel 2:1-2).

In the Old Testament, the judgment of 'the day of the Lord' was pronounced against God's enemies (Zeph. 3:8-12; Joel 3:14-16; Obad. 15-17; Zech. 12:8-9), and God's people (Joel 1:15-20; Amos 5:18;

Zeph. 1:7-18). Basically, it spoke of judgment on sin, and victory for the Lord's cause (Joel 2:31-32). In Zephaniah (1:14-18) the tempo of God's warning builds up so that the 'great day of the Lord' is said to be coming swiftly. It is pictured in a seven-fold way, as:

- **a day of distress (v.15,17)**
- **a day of devastation (v.15)**
- **a day of desolation (v.15)**
- **a day of darkness (v.15)**
- **a day of death (v.17)**
- **a day of devouring (v.18), and**
- **a day of despair (v.18), for nothing 'shall be able to deliver them.'**

God has never grown accustomed to sin. In contrast to human beings, he has never learned to tolerate it. He is holy, and has consistently hated all that is contrary to his pure and sinless character. Nations and people proudly shake their fist in the face of God, refusing him and saying, in effect, 'We do not want you to reign over us.' God, in his perfect timing, will bring this to an end. Worldlings will be staggered, because they will complacently feel that there is peace and safety, when in fact God is about to bring sudden destruction.

There is a sense of awful suspense in Paul's vivid use of words: sudden / comes / destruction. Destruction does not refer to annihilation, but to everlasting, hopeless 'lostness' in hell (see Dan. 12:2; Matt. 25:46; Mark 9:44,46,48; Luke 16:19-31; 2 Thess. 1:8,9; Rev. 14:10; 20:10). In our day particularly we need to emphasize that there are no alternatives to heaven or hell, to life with the Lord or lostness apart from him. One or the other is inevitable. If we take seriously the solemn warnings concerning judgment to come, let us earnestly warn people of their urgent need to get right with God while there is still time.

> No tears for England?
> Lord, I pray,
> Oh, melt my callous heart today;
> Burn in my soul the awful doom
> Of those unsaved beyond the tomb.
>
> Lance Pibworth

Verses 5-11

You are all sons of light and sons of the day. We are not of the night nor of darkness. Therefore let us not sleep, as others do, but let us watch and be sober. For those who sleep, sleep at night, and those who get drunk are drunk at night. But let us who are of the day be sober, putting on the breastplate of faith and love, and as a helmet the hope of salvation. For God did not appoint us to wrath, but to obtain salvation through our Lord Jesus Christ, who died for us, that whether we wake or sleep, we should live together with Him. Therefore comfort each other and edify one another, just as you also are doing.

Christians can eagerly look forward to the time of Christ's return. God will be seen to be true and his righteousness will reign. There is no condemnation to those who are in Christ Jesus (Romans 8:1), but 'the day' (1 Cor. 3:13-14) will reveal the true nature of our Christian lives. Our eternal destiny is already settled. If we are saved we will be in heaven with Christ for ever. If our work as believers endures we will receive a reward. Taken into account on that day will be:

- ◆ our testimony for Christ (Phil. 2:16)
- ◆ our suffering for Christ (1 Pet. 4:13)
- ◆ our faithfulness to Christ (Luke 12:42-43; Rev. 2:10)

- ◆ our service for Christ (1 Cor. 9:6; 1 Tim. 6:17-19)
- ◆ our use of time for Christ (Eph. 5:15-16; Col. 4:5)
- ◆ our exercise of spiritual gifts (Matt. 25:14-28; 1 Pet. 4:10)
- ◆ our self-discipline for Christ (1 Cor. 9:24-25)
- ◆ our leading souls to Christ (1 Thess. 2:19)

Any rewards are entirely according to God's mercy. He has given us life and talent. More than that, he has saved us through the sacrificial death of his dear Son. He has forgiven us, come to live within us by his Holy Spirit, and even been willing to use us. Then he rewards us for serving him. God is indeed full of grace! As sons of the light, let us be armed, awake and alert (vv.6-8), waiting for the day of the Lord's return.

Verses 6-7
Therefore let us not sleep, as others do, but let us watch and be sober. For those who sleep, sleep at night, and those who get drunk are drunk at night.

In the light of Christ's second coming we should wake up. Time is a daily treasure which attracts many robbers. This is not the moment to be half asleep. We should be discerning the times, be aware of the seasons, in full control of our senses, and alert so that we can do what God asks of us. Obviously Paul's teaching is metaphorical—we need sleep, though we shouldn't be getting drunk! Sleep and drunkenness picture a state in which a person is dull and open to surprise. Rather, we are to be alert and awake. Daily reading of the Bible will help us to act with understanding as good judges of the times. Having the Lord's insights, we can have clearer understanding of what is happening in the world than even the greatest politicians.

It is all too easy to be blown about with 'winds of doctrine'. Some of these may come from within the church, others from the world, and others may have Satanic origins. The Bible is our final authority in all matters of faith and doctrine. Imagine sitting on a railway train. You look out of the window and see the train standing next to you begin to move. Then you wonder if it is your carriage moving, but you are not sure. What do you do? You quickly look at the platform, and find that it is stationary (Hmm!). Now you look back at the other carriage to see clearly that it is moving. The Bible is our platform. It is truth unchanged and unchanging. We judge everything by what it teaches, so we need to be very familiar with its message. I urge us all to be in the daily, dogged, but delightful discipline of meeting with the Lord. This 4-D quiet time will become such a blessing to you, as well as a guide to your life.

Verses 8-9

But let us who are of the day be sober, putting on the breastplate of faith and love, and as a helmet the hope of salvation. For God did not appoint us to wrath, but to obtain salvation through our Lord Jesus Christ,

Notice in this verse the trinity of faith, hope and love again. Paul says that these things can be 'put on'. The idea reminds us of Ephesians 6 where we read about putting on the whole armour of God. Frances Ridley Havergal says, 'each piece put on with prayer'. As an act of obedience to God we can by faith dress ourselves in spiritual armour ready for the battle of the day ahead. Being equipped for battle is part of watchfulness. 'Watch, stand fast in the faith, be brave, be strong. Let all that you do be done in love' (1 Cor. 16:13,14).

The uncertainty, on our part, as to the day and the hour of the Lord's return is sufficient reason for alertness, but with enemies of the faith around us and the command to be spiritually earnest, the need for watchfulness is quite clear. One author says, 'The sober person lives deeply. His pleasures are not primarily those of the senses, like the pleasures of the drunkard . . . but those of the soul.'

72

Thankfully, the Christian has been delivered from wrath through the Lord Jesus. Salvation is of the Lord, and it is also our inheritance as his sons and daughters. Salvation is both negative and positive—the saved person is rescued from the guilt and punishment of sin, but also has numerous spiritual benefits and blessings which come from the open hand of God who loves to lavish on his children all that will be for their good and his glory. Our hope of salvation is certain, for God has appointed us not to wrath (as he has all who refuse his rule) but to receive salvation in all its final fulness at the return of our Lord Jesus Christ.

Verses 10-11

Who died for us, that whether we wake or sleep, we should live together with Him. Therefore comfort each other and edify one another, just as you also are doing.

G. Harding Wood breaks up this section under three headings:

- **the Thessalonian Christians in relation to the heathen (vv.6-10)**
- **The Thessalonian Christians in relation to one another (vv.11-15)**
- **the Thessalonian Christians individually (vv.16-24)**

When considering the salvation which Christ bought for us, the Christian can feel, 'I have been bought with a price; I am not my own; I want to live for Christ at all times; I want to proclaim him whether in season or out of season.' Whether awake or asleep, alive or dead, all believers will live together with Christ. There is an implication in the writing of this letter that someone in the Thessalonian church had died, and Paul wants to comfort the church concerning this departed, loved believer (see 4:13; 5:10). I have been to funerals of the unsaved and of real believers. What a difference there is. However, every bereavement does bring with it a sense of loss. Like an amputation, you can learn to live with the loss, but you are never the same again.

God is fair and just. 'Power belongs to God. Also to You, O Lord, belongs mercy; for You render to each one according to his work' (Ps. 62:11,12). The thought of Christ's second coming gives great consolation when the troubles of the world seem overwhelming. Jesus' return to this earth is more for comfort than controversy. It edifies and encourages flagging Christians, giving the assurance that God will sort out all things one day.

Verses 12-15

And we urge you, brethren, to recognise those who labour among you, and are over you in the Lord and admonish you, and to esteem them very highly in love for their work's sake. Be at peace among yourselves. Now we exhort you, brethren, warn those who are unruly, comfort the fainthearted, uphold the weak, be patient with all. See that no one renders evil for evil to anyone, but always pursue what is good both for yourselves and for all.

Here, we see Paul urging the Thessalonians from the very depth of his heart to be godly in their attitude to each other. He again calls the Christians, brethren. It is his favourite name for Christians—he uses it more than sixty times in his letters and twenty-seven times in 1 and 2 Thessalonians. The fruit of the Spirit, as listed in Galatians 5:22,23 comes to mind in this passage, for we read of love (v.13), joy (v.16), peace (v.13) and long-suffering (v.14).

Authority is not to be despised. National and local government has authority over civilians, employers have authority in the workplace, parents have authority over their children, and leaders in the church have authority there. Pastors, elders, deacons and officers each have their role and are to be respected as such. The 'peril of the pendulum' can be very evident in church life. Neither the extreme of every voice in church being adhered to, nor of a pastor or leader having final sway in all things is helpful or right. We all need checks and balances. Every ministry needs to be accountable to faithful friends who can honestly and lovingly correct imbalances. Peter wrote, 'Shepherd the flock of God which is among you, serving as overseers, not by constraint but willingly, not for dishonest gain but eagerly; nor as being lords over those entrusted to you but being examples to the flock' (1 Peter 5:2-3). Humility will characterize good and godly leadership.

Was Paul redressing a balance when he urged the Thessalonians 'to recognise those who labour among you, and are over you in the Lord and admonish you'? He instructs them to esteem them highly in love for their work's sake. Where leaders are not lording it over the flock of God, but lovingly feeding them with his word, we must beware that we do not find ourselves murmuring against the leadership which God has appointed them to exercise. Pray specifically for Christian leaders, seek to be a blessing to them and, as much as is possible, learn to overlook their faults. Christian leaders often find themselves either on the top of things or on the bottom under them, respected or hated, the hero or the villain, admired or criticized—on the yo-yo of Christian opinion. They are, like us, all human, having their own individual needs for strength and encouragement.

I came across a little piece entitled, 'Who changed?'

There was once a preacher whom I used to like;
I thought he was great;
His sermons were wonderful
As long as I liked them.
His speech was fair,
His life was clean,
He was a hard worker—
As long as I liked him
He was the man for the job,

In fact I was strong for him,
As long as I liked him
But he offended me one day—
Whether he knew it or not, I don't know.
Since that day he has ceased to be a good preacher;
His sermons aren't so wonderful—
Since he offended me.
His speech isn't so good,
His faults are more prominent,
Since he offended me.
He's not a hard worker—
In fact he's really not the man for the job—
Since he offended me.
It's really a shame he's changed so much to me.

—Author unknown

Verse 13

And to esteem them very highly in love for their work's sake. Be at peace among yourselves.

The 'peace' referred to here is freedom from opposition. Jesus said, 'Blessed are the peacemakers' (Matt. 5:9). Paul concluded his second letter to the Corinthians saying, '. . . be of one mind, live in peace; and the God of love and peace will be with you . . .' (13:11). Similarly, as he concluded his letter to the Romans (12:18), he said, 'If it is possible, as much as depends on you, live peaceably with all men.' We are to live at peace, because God is a God of peace, and Christ who is the Prince of Peace is honoured as we do so.

When tempted to judge or condemn other Christians, let us remember:

◆ we may not be in possession of all the evidence
◆ the time for the final 'trial' has not yet come
◆ if we do judge, we ourselves will be judged (Matt. 7:1)
◆ a higher tribunal has been appointed.

Never take sides without fully hearing each point of view. Be very wary to 'write off' a brother or sister on the grounds of what others have said about them. Do your utmost to speak well of people, and faithfully pray for those you find most difficult. Life is too short to fritter away on squabbles. If the Lord has treated us with great mercy, shouldn't we therefore, do the same to others, even if they have hurt us? Take down the pictures on your dartboard, renounce your grudges, tear up your hate list, and live at peace with all. Jesus said, 'If you bring your gift to altar, and there remember that your brother has something against you, leave your gift there before the altar and go your way. First be reconciled to your brother, and then come and offer your gift' (Matt. 5:23-24). Am I a peacemaker or a trouble maker?

Verses 14-15
Now we exhort you, brethren, warn those who are unruly, comfort the fainthearted, uphold the weak, be patient with all. See that no one renders evil for evil to anyone, but always pursue what is good both for yourselves and for all.

Are there unruly or idle people in your church? I am sure you are not one!! The disorderly who are out of step with the word of God are to be warned and admonished. Every believer has enough 'flesh' in him or her to be able to wreck a church. Sometimes those who you would imagine would know better can be the most dangerous. Leadership has at times to 'grasp the nettle' and deal with situations that could lead to disaster. Failure to do so can lead to much greater problems. The balance between firm and decisive leadership which allows individual Christians freedom and individuality is not easy, but vital in a day when too many churches and Christians are 'doing their own thing'.

Comfort the fainthearted. Seek to say a word of cheer and encourage-ment to those who lack confidence and are nervous about life. Many

77

a soul is wounded; their dreams have become shattered, hopes disappointed, and loneliness often dominates their desire to be joyful and vigorous. It is so encouraging that such people often find real help in the Christian family. Sitting next to them in church, showing genuine concern about their needs, passing on a thought from the Bible, and helping them practically, and showing hospitality to them can be ways of obeying this command. It is amazing how far a smile, an affirming word or even a gentle touch will go.

Uphold the weak again underlines that we are to help and support the physically, mentally and spiritually weak. The real calibre of a church can be seen in how its members treat the mentally disabled, the deaf, the physically handicapped, the blind, those in wheelchairs, or those who simply need added patience if we are to meet their needs. There are so many needs, and so many doors of opportunity to minister. In caring for such, we earn the right to take the opportunity to point them to Christ. Let us not forget that David needed a Jonathan, Elijah an Elisha and even Paul had Epaphras, Luke, Onesiphorus and Epaphroditus.

Be at peace and *be patient* are two commands which are blood relatives. There are many in our churches, who are not good at communication, who are not bright, vivacious or even attractive and whose company we would rather avoid. Nevertheless, they were made by God (Exod. 4:11), loved by God, are part of the body of Christ, the church (1 Cor. 12:14-25), and for whom God has his purposes (Eph. 2:10). Who then are we to be too busy for such people? Each is precious in his sight. Perhaps we reveal more about ourselves than we care to think when we are choosy about those for whom we have time and attention. Remember, love suffers long and is kind. What a big, encompassing word is made of these three letters spelling 'all'! *Be patient with all.*

Blind songwriter, Ken Medema describes this loving quality which churches should display, in his song 'If this is not a place':

If this is not a place where tears are understood,
Then where shall I go to cry?
And if this is not a place where my spirit can take wings,
Then where shall I go to fly?

I don't need another place for tryin' to impress you
With just how good and virtuous I am, no, no, no.
I don't need another place for always bein' on top of things,
Everybody knows that it's a sham, it's a sham.
I don't need another place for always wearin' smiles,
Even when it's not the way I feel.
I don't need another place to mouth the same old platitudes.
Everybody knows that it's not real.

So if this is not a place where my questions can be asked,
Then where shall I go to seek?
And if this is not a place where my heart cry can be heard,
Where, tell me where, shall I go to speak?

So if this is not a place where tears are understood,
Where shall I go, where shall I go to fly?

In contrast to the love Christians should know and show, bitterness springs up like a cancer and can destroy the inward joy and freedom which ought to be ours as Christians. It arises because we feel that some right of ours has been violated, but as Christians we have no rights—we have yielded them to God. The emphasis of our lives ought to be on our responsibilities rather than our rights. This excludes revenge, grudges and vindictiveness. We are not to render evil for evil, but learn to be meek, turning the other cheek, and seeking to help those who curse us. What a striking contrast this is to the world, which insists on its own way, and on fair treatment! They did not treat the Lord Jesus like that, and yet his submission has led to blessing for the whole world. When Christ was reviled, he did not revile in return. Like a lamb, he was silent before his shearers. He prayed for those who crucified him, forgave the dying, cursing thief, re-commissioned Peter who denied him, and revealed himself to Thomas who doubted him. He took, cleansed and so greatly used Saul of Tarsus, who had helped in the execution of Stephen. Dare we be less loving than he has been to even me?

Rather than repay evil for evil, we are instructed actively and always to pursue what is good. Augustine said, 'Good for good, evil for evil: that is natural. Evil for good: that is devilish. Good for evil: that is divine.' It sounds almost humanistic to say that we should look for the good in people, but we can at least try to imagine what a person might be if he or she submitted to the goodness and grace of God for forgiveness and new life. Pursuing good conjures up the idea of purposeful activity as we look around earnestly wanting to impart blessing and help to all and sundry. Oh, for more of us to be like that, and to do all for the glory of God. Where we can let us help (financially, socially and practically) those who are seeking to do good, especially to those who lend a helping hand in the name of Christ.

To recap verses 12-15, we see that:

- **leaders are to be appreciated**
- **believers are to be united**
- **disorderly Christians are to be warned**
- **fainthearted people are to be cheered**
- **weak brothers and sisters are to be encouraged**
- **all and sundry are to be treated with patience**
- **everyone is someone to whom we can do good.**

Verses 16-22

Rejoice always, pray without ceasing, in everything give thanks; for this is the will of God in Christ Jesus for you. Do not quench the Spirit. Do not despise prophecies. Test all things; hold fast what is good. Abstain from every form of evil.

Now may the God of peace Himself sanctify you completely; and may your whole spirit, soul, and body be preserved blameless at the coming of our Lord Jesus Christ. He who calls you is faithful, who also will do it. Brethren, pray for us. Greet all the brethren with a holy kiss. I charge you by the Lord that this epistle be read to all the holy brethren. The grace of our Lord Jesus Christ be with you. Amen.

As far as the unconverted world is concerned, we are to be separate from their ways, yet seeking to draw alongside them and win them to Christ (vv.6-10). As far as other believers are concerned, we are to be united (vv.11-15). We are to be very practical in the way we obey the Lord and openly show our relationship with him. There is here a description of the frame of mind Christians ought to have. It is to be:

- **joyful (v.16)**
- **prayerful (v.17**
- **thankful (v.18**
- **spiritual (v.19)**
- **teachable (v.20)**
- **judicial (v.21)**
- **honourable (v.22)**

In essence, we want the type of mind which was in Christ Jesus (Phil. 2:5ff.).

We are to *rejoice evermore* and to give thanks in everything. Our spirit is to express the joy of our soul. Not everyone has the same personality, but all Christians ought to be able to show the deep gratitude they have towards God. We have been saved! We are on our way to heaven! We are children of the King of kings. Christ is coming again. We will be rejoicing in heaven, so let's get in tune and practise now.

Verse 17
Pray without ceasing.

There is more wisdom found in the three words of verse 17 than in all the words of the greatest of the world's philosophers. *Pray without ceasing.* I seek to begin each day with prayer, and I recommend this holy habit to you. But this verse is saying more. It is teaching an attitude that leads us to be in constant contact with God: to quickly confess our sins to the Lord (keep short accounts with God), to be constantly thankful, and automatically turning the needs we see around into prayer. Praying is not easy. When we pray we are engaging in warfare against principalities and powers. We need to learn to pray 'in the Spirit' (Eph. 6:18).

Billy Graham said, 'Noah prayed and God handed him the blue print of the ark of deliverance. Moses prayed and God delivered the Israelites from Egyptian bondage. Gideon prayed, and the host of a formidable army fled in fear before his valiant, prayerful three hundred. Daniel prayed, and the mouths of the lions were closed. The disciples prayed, and they were filled with the Holy Spirit so that 3,000 were added to the church in one day. Paul prayed and hundreds of churches were born in Asia Minor and Europe. God does answer prayer.'

The Bible teaches, 'The effectual fervent prayer of a righteous man avails much' (Jas. 5:16). The Puritans used to say about prayer, 'Descend to the particular.' We must pray specifically, and if we ask anything according to God's will, he will hear us. The Lord always longs to hear us pray, so the scope for our prayers and petitions is unlimited. The lesson is clear—we are to pray!

Pray for others; pray for the lost; pray for your family; pray for your own needs; dare I write it?—please pray for me, but above all, PRAY! 'Whatever things you ask when you pray, believe that you will receive them, and you will have them' (Mark 11:24). 'Continue earnestly in prayer, being vigilant in it with thanksgiving' (Col. 4:2).

Verse 18

In everything give thanks; for this is the will of God in Christ Jesus for you.

In chapter 4:3, we read that the will of God for us is our sanctification. Now we learn that the will of God is that in everything we are to give thanks. Thankfulness is an expression of the sanctified soul. An attitude of gratitude is an aid to sanctification. Saying grace before meals provides a good, regular opportunity to briefly stop and return thanks to God for his provision. Ministering in Communist Poland in the mid-1980s, I was moved by a group of Christian young people with whom I had gone to a restaurant for a meal. Undaunted by political fears, they stood and reverently sang grace before enjoying their meal. For them, thanksgiving became an opportunity to witness to their faith. In a cynical and ungrateful world, thankfulness is in itself a stark testimony to our love for the Lord.

Matthew Henry, the great Bible commentator was, on one occasion, robbed by highwaymen. He wrote in his diary that day, 'Let me be thankful—first, because I was never robbed before; second, because although they took my wallet, they did not take my life; third, because although they took my all, it was not too much; and fourth, because it was I who was robbed, not I who did the robbing!'

In a similar vein, William Carey, missionary to India, experienced painful loss whilst away from his home base. A fire broke out and completely destroyed the building, the presses, many Bibles, and the precious manuscripts, dictionaries and grammars which he had prepared for the use of his successors. When he returned and was told of the tragic loss, he showed no sign of despair or impatience. Instead, he knelt and thanked God that he still had the strength to do the work over again. He started immediately, not wasting time on self-pity. Before his death, he had duplicated and improved on his earlier achievements. (Take note all we who have lost work on our computers!)

Paul could testify that he had learned that in whatever state he was to be content. Let us not forget we have more than we deserve; we have been treated better than we deserve; we have lived longer than we deserve, and one day, we are going to heaven. There is plenty for which to thank God.

Joyful, prayerful and thankful is the Bible's order. Even in prison, Paul kept joyfully praying and thanking (Acts 16). Jesus was supremely all three. He is always our perfect pattern. Recognize his closeness to you in every situation, and you will find that his joy, intercession and thankfulness are infectious.

Verse 19
Do not quench the Spirit.

The Holy Spirit, whose supreme mission is to point people to the Lord Jesus Christ, has been the subject of debate and division. It is he who unites believers in love for Christ and each other, but Christians have been guilty of abusing his gentle ministry. The Bible's commands concerning the Holy Spirit reveal aspects of his attributes: 'do not grieve the Spirit'—he is a Person; 'do not resist the Spirit'—he is a Power; 'Do not quench the Spirit'—he is like fire. What is it that can quench the Spirit? We can quench the Spirit by:

◆ *sinning*—remember he is the Holy Spirit, and without holiness, we cannot see the Lord.

84

- *tradition*—we are not revolutionaries wanting to overthrow traditions, but they can become a burden which is heavy to bear, holding us back from freely serving the Lord.

- *man-made rules*—we have our own self-imposed limits of what we do or do not do, but if they are not directly stated in the Bible we have no right to impose them on others, or judge those who disagree with us.

- *mechanical worship*—the people who lead corporate worship, as well as we individuals in our quiet times with the Lord, must be sensitive to the Lord's leading, and seek to be relevant to the situation of souls at that particular time.

- *disunity*—how can a group be at one with the Holy Spirit if there is bitterness or fighting between us? The same Holy Spirit dwells in all believers, and we should seek oneness of heart and spirit. It is the height of insults to squabble over the doctrine of the Spirit.

- *silence*—when there is the opportunity to speak of Christ to others.

Practically, is there anything at all in our lives, which quenches the Holy Spirit? We have the daily choice as children of God to either resist the Spirit, or submit to him, grieve the Spirit or please him, quench the Holy Spirit, or allow him to be the fire in our lives.

George Matheson, has added another insight to this verse. He said: 'There is a thirst which ought not to be quenched—the thirst for God. It is like no other thirst in the world . . . If I do not taste of God I shall cease to thirst for Him; the Spirit will be quenched.'

Verses 20-21
Do not despise prophecies. Test all things; hold fast what is good.

'Do not despise prophecies.' We must remember that this letter was one of the first that the apostle Paul wrote. The early church did not have a New Testament at the time this letter was written, there was little Christian literature, and comparatively few hymns. In these early days before our Bible was complete, there were prophets such as Agabus (Acts 21:10-11; *cf*.13:1-3) who could speak directly from God. Their gifts, authenticity and authority was recognized in the church. Such people and messages were not to be despised.

Today, we have Bible teachers who teach the word of God, as written in the pages of the Bible. We must be careful not to despise such people. Referring to Old Testament worship, Solomon said, 'Walk prudently when you go to the house of God . . .' (Eccles. 5:1). If we do not despise prophecies, we will listen attentively to the word expounded and taught; we will not grumble about the length of a sermon; we will not just pick out our favourite preachers; we will closely follow, with an open Bible, what is being preached; perhaps we will take notes, for the recording of a truth deepens the impression it makes on us; we will talk about and meditate over the things heard; we will love to hear God's word proclaimed; we will want everyone to hear the word; we will want to hear as many messages as we possibly can.

Perhaps our nation has been guilty of despising prophecies, and therefore we are in the situation Amos warned about: 'Behold the days are coming, says the Lord God, that I will send a famine on the land, not a famine of bread, nor a thirst for water, but of hearing the words of the Lord' (8:11). Hudson Taylor said, 'There is a living God. He has spoken in the Bible. He means what He says, and will do all He has promised.' Is it possible, therefore, for us to have too high a view of God's preached word?

We must remember that all 'messages from God' have to be carefully scrutinized and tested by the plumb line standard of the Bible. I have been 'given' words which were supposed to be from God, but as time passed, it clearly demonstrated that they were not from the Lord who never makes mistakes (see Deut. 18:20-22). We need the gift of discernment today. Simply because a godly person says something does not necessarily mean it is right. There is a sad story in 1 Kings 13 of a 'man of God' misleading another messenger of God, culminating in his physical death. Jeremiah 23:16-40 warns us of false prophets who claim to have a message from heaven, but their thoughts, sermons and dreams were man-made, and manipulated the people of God. Beware of wolves in sheep's clothing—they wear genuine wool! Matthew 24:11; 2 Peter and Jude, as well as 1 Timothy 4:1-6 need to be carefully studied and noted in these days. Promptings and advice from others can be helpful, but God speaks today through the Bible.

Wrong beliefs and wrong behaviour are linked. If we let our biblical principles slip, bad practices will follow. After idolatry comes immorality; after ungodliness comes unrighteousness. Therefore, after Paul has said 'test all things' he immediately says, 'hold fast what is good'. Hold tenaciously to everything that is right about what you believe and what you do, and don't allow laziness, busy-ness or pressure from others to deter you from continuing these faithful practices.

Verse 22
Abstain from every form of evil.

When the possibility of sin was presented to Joseph, he fled. We know from Genesis 39 something of the power of temptation and what it cost Joseph to refuse to yield, but he kept his purity and integrity.

At the very appearance of evil—even if it looks a long way from us—we are better to run and escape than become ensnared. Let us not give wrong impressions by what we do. Professor Verna Wright, to whom I have dedicated this book, puts the idea this way: 'Don't fasten your shoelaces in a strawberry field!' We wouldn't want people to think we are stealing strawberries. I understand that Billy Graham will only drink milk when involved in a television interview, so that all may see that he is not drinking alcohol. We are to avoid all kinds of evil. What is tempting to one, may not be to another, but we wouldn't want to be a stumbling-block to weaker brothers, so we are to be careful for their sake. Cut out everything which is harmful, but hold on to that which is good.

God is holy. He consistently hates sin, and as we draw closer to him, we will hate it more and more as well. Dr Robert G. Lee has said: 'God looks on sin and sinning as you would look on a dagger that pierced your mother's heart as it was thrust therein by the hand of a murderer—with righteous revulsion. God looks on sin as you would look on a rattlesnake if you found it coiled in your baby's bed—with holy hate. God looks on sin as you would look on the vulture that would pick out the eyes of your darling child and leave it blind the rest of its days. God looks on sin as you would look on a buzzard in your dining room. God looks on sin as you would look on the finger prints of the lust demon on the lily-white throat of your fair daughter. God looks on sin as you would look on the footprint of your home's burglar. God hates sin. The Bethlehem manger says so. The thorns on His brow and the nails in His hands and the spear in His side and the blood on His cheek and chin and knee, blood in drops, blood in rills, blood in pools at the foot of the cross—all these say so! The empty tomb in the garden says so.'

There is balance in the Christian life. This little section ends on a negative—abstain; the next section is very positive—may the God of peace sanctify you completely. There are certain things I will not do as a Christian, but there are other activities I deliberately get involved in because I am a Christian. Just as I do not put extra petrol in an already full tank, I do not need endlessly to pursue my own happiness, for God will provide me with numerous joys which are not displeasing to himself.

Verse 23
Now may the God of peace Himself sanctify you completely; and may your whole spirit, soul, and body be preserved blameless at the coming of our Lord Jesus Christ.

The climax of Paul's letter, is a prayer for the church he loves so much. He has told them that he prays for them, now he tells us what exactly is his prayer for them. F. F. Bruce calls this a 'wish-prayer'. Chuck Swindoll says, 'In a sense, Paul is praying with his eyes open and looking directly at his dear friends.' He wants them to be sanctified, set aside for God's holy service. We will never be sinless this side of heaven, but we should aim and pray that, in Murray McCheyne's words, God would make us as holy as a saved sinner can be. Every part of our personality will need to be brought under the control of the God of peace. (At least six times in the New Testament God is called, 'the God of peace'—see Romans 15:33; 16:20; 2 Cor. 13:11; Phil. 4:9; 1 Thess. 5:23; Heb. 13:20.)

The world puts the body first, then the soul and finally the spirit. That is not the order here. The spirit (that part of us which can know, worship, appreciate and enjoy God), the soul (our true character and person) and body are all to be preserved blameless, not just for a few years, but until the time the Lord Jesus rends the heavens and returns to earth. Every corner of my being needs to be purified.

This prayer actually brings together the major themes of the whole letter. It is a prayer which is pertinent to the needs of the Thessalonians.

They needed the preservation of the:

◆ *spirit* from everything that takes away assurance (1 :5; 2:13), that distracts us (3:5), and that prevents true worship (1:9).

◆ *soul* from discouragement and a sense of hopelessness (3:2-3), from contention and strife (3:12), and from evil thoughts (4:5).

◆ *body* from defilement (5:15), from evil uses (4:3,6), and from laziness (4:11,12; 5:6).

Pray this prayer for your church, Christian friends, family, and for yourself.

Verses 24-28

He who calls you is faithful, who also will do it. Brethren, pray for us. Greet all the brethren with a holy kiss. I charge you by the Lord that this epistle be read to all the holy brethren. The grace of our Lord Jesus Christ be with you. Amen.

Having prayed specific prayers for the Thessalonians, Paul is assured that the Lord will hear and answer. What God asks of us, he will enable us to do, and be with us in the doing of it.

Paul is not ashamed to ask others to pray for him. He does this in at least seven of his letters. To fail to pray for other believers is sin (1 Sam. 12:23). We need each other's prayers. I have sometimes wondered if, like Elijah, a widow woman (the type of person who will never hit the headlines of the Christian press) has sustained me by her prayers.

The holy kiss greeting was not a sensual thing. In today's western society for a man to kiss any other woman than his wife is an appearance of evil, not love. The practice has become popular in some Christian circles today, and to be honest, I don't like it. The *Living Bible* paraphrase seems more appropriate for our age, where it is all too easy to stumble: 'Shake hands for me with all the brothers there.'

The Old Testament was read in the synagogues. (You remember that this is where Paul began his ministry in Thessalonica for the space of three Sabbaths—Acts 17:1-10. This was his usual strategy—beginning in the synagogues, he preached until he was rejected, and then he moved to the Gentiles. The first converts in a city, at least, would have some grasp of the Scriptures.) Now Paul asks that this epistle be read out loud to all the holy (that is how God sees us in grace) brethren. There is great value in listening to the Word of God read out loud.

The epistle began with 'grace' (1:1), now it is to end on the same theme. The Christian gospel is all of grace—from beginning to end. James Denney says: 'Whatever God has to say to us—and in all the New Testament letters there are things that search the heart and make it quake—begins and ends with grace . . . All that God has been to man in Jesus Christ is summed up in it: all His gentleness and patience, all the holy passion of His love, is gathered up in grace. What could one soul wish for another than that the grace of the Lord Jesus Christ should be with it?'

The letter is written to encourage a persecuted church. Paul does not rebuke its members but urges that they increase more and more in their love and obedience. He esteemed the concerns of the Thessalonians greater than his own. He wrote responding to their needs rather than his own. His encouraging words prompt us to evaluate what our own struggles really are. Every chapter ends on the theme of the second coming of Christ. This is the ultimate encouragement. For considering the return of Christ, we are encouraging ourselves in the Lord (see 1 Sam. 30:6b), and in turn receiving strength to live for him each new day. One day he will come, and all we have been through here on earth will be worth it when we see Jesus.

'He who testifies to these things says, 'Surely I am coming quickly.' Amen. Even so, come, Lord Jesus! The grace of our Lord Jesus Christ be with you all. Amen' (Rev. 22:20-21).

Be encouraged!